DIMESTORE

Also by Lee Smith

NOVELS

The Last Day the Dogbushes Bloomed

Something in the Wind

Fancy Strut

Black Mountain Breakdown

Oral History

Family Linen

Fair and Tender Ladies

The Devil's Dream

Saving Grace

The Christmas Letters

The Last Girls

On Agate Hill

Guests on Earth

STORY COLLECTIONS

Cakewalk

Me and My Baby View the Eclipse

News of the Spirit

Mrs. Darcy and the Blue-Eyed Stranger

NONFICTION, EDITED WITH INTRODUCTION

Sitting on the Courthouse Bench

An Oral History of Grundy, Virginia

DIMESTORE

LEE SMITH

ALGONQUIN BOOKS OF CHAPEL HILL   2016

Published by
ALGONQUIN BOOKS OF CHAPEL HILL
Post Office Box 2225
Chapel Hill, North Carolina 27515-2225

a division of
WORKMAN PUBLISHING
225 Varick Street
New York, New York 10014

"Dimestore" contains material by Lee Smith from two articles from the *Washington Post* and the introduction to *Sitting on the Courthouse Bench: An Oral History of Grudy, Virginia,* edited by Lee Smith, 2000, Tryon Publishing Co., Chapel Hill, N.C.

"Recipe Box," originally published in *House and Garden,* 2002.

"Lady Lessons" in *Garden and Gun,* 2010.

A version of "Marble Cake," in *Eudora Welty: Writers' Reflections upon First Reading Welty,* edited by Pearl McHaney, originally published by Hill Street Press, 1999.

"Raised to Leave," in the *Washington Post Sunday Magazine,* 2001.

"Lightning Storm," originally published by the *New York Times* as "Given Tools, They Work the Language," 1996.

"Driving Miss Daisy Crazy," originally a talk, then published as the introduction to *New Stories from the South,* 2001.

"Good-bye to the Sunset Man," originally published in the *Independent Weekly,* October 2004.

"A Life in Books," based on an Associated Writing Program keynote address (and then printed in the AWP magazine/newsletter) and a piece named "Everything Else Falls Away" written for the collection *Why I Write: Thoughts on the Craft of Fiction,* edited by Will Blythe, Little, Brown, 1998.

"Angels Passing," originally published in the *Independent Weekly.*

"The Little Locksmith," in the *Raleigh News and Observer,* 2002.

"Heritage," in *From the Mountain, From the Valley: New and Collected Poems* by James Still, edited by Ted Olson, published by the University Press of Kentucky, March 2005.

Excerpts from *The Wolfpen Notebooks: A Record of Appalachian Life* by James Still, published by the University Press of Kentucky, July 9, 1991.

"Salvation," in *The River Hills and Beyond* by Lou Crabtree, published by Sow's Ear Press, 1998.

"Song to Oysters," in *Soupsongs/Webster's Ark* by Roy Blount Jr., published by Houghton Mifflin, 1987.

With gratitude to the original publishers of Lee Smith's work quoted herein: *The Last Day the Dogbushes Bloomed,* Harper and Row, New York, 1968. *Oral History* (1983) and *Fair and Tender Ladies* (1988), G. P. Putnam's Sons, New York. The story "Tongues of Fire," in *Me and My Baby View the Eclipse,* by Lee Smith, G. P. Putnam's Sons, New York, 1990.

LIBRARY OF CONGRESS CATALOGING-IN-PUBLICATION DATA
Smith, Lee, [date]
Dimestore : a writer's life / Lee Smith.
pages cm
ISBN 978-1-61620-502-7
1. Smith, Lee, [date]—Childhood and youth. 2. Grundy (Va.)—Biography.
3. Grundy (Va.)—Social life and customs. I. Title.
F234.G84S62 2016
975.5′752—dc23   2015023739

10 9 8 7 6 5 4 3 2 1

First Edition

For my grandchildren,
Lucy, Spencer, Ellery, and Baker

Writing fiction has developed in me an abiding respect for the unknown in a human lifetime and a sense of where to look for the threads, how to follow, how to connect, find in the thick of the tangle what clear line persists. The strands are all there: to the memory nothing is ever really lost.

The events in our lives happen in a sequence in time, but in their significance to ourselves they find their own order, a timetable not necessarily—perhaps not possibly—chronological. The time as we know it subjectively is often the chronology that stories and novels follow: it is the continuous thread of revelation.

—*One Writer's Beginnings,* Eudora Welty

CONTENTS

Raised to Leave:
Some Thoughts on "Culture"

I WAS BORN IN A RUGGED RING of mountains in southwest Virginia—mountains so high, so straight up and down, that the sun didn't even hit our yard until about eleven o'clock. My uncle Bob Venable—they lived across the road—used to predict the weather by sticking his head out the window and hollering back inside, "Sun on the mountaintop, girls!" to my cousins. The only flat land in the county lay in a narrow band along the river where we lived, about a mile from town. Though we all ate out of the garden, real farming was impossible in that hard rock ground. The only thing it produced was coal. We never thought of our jagged mountains as scenic, either, though we all played up in them every day after school. We never saw a tourist, and nobody we knew hiked for fun.

I will never forget the first time I ever saw a jogger: my mother and I were sitting on the front porch stringing beans and watching the cars go up and down Route 460 in front of our house, when suddenly one of these VISTAs we'd been hearing about, a long-haired boy with great legs, came running right up the road. We both stood up, and watched him run out of sight. "Well, for heaven's sakes," my mother said. "Where do you reckon he's going, running like that?"

He was going back to where he came from, eventually; but most of us weren't going anyplace. We were closed in entirely, cut off from the outside world by our ring of mountains. Many of the children I went to school with had never been out of Buchanan County. People still described my own mother as "not from around here," though she had spent most of her life teaching their children and "trying to civilize you and your daddy!" as she always joked, but it was a challenge.

So I was being raised to leave.

I WAS NOT TO USE double negatives; I was not to say "me and Martha." I was not to trade my pimento cheese sandwiches at school for the lunch I really wanted: cornbread and buttermilk in a mason jar, brought by the kids from the hollers. Me and Martha were not to play in the black river behind our house, dirty with coal that would stain my shorts. I was to take piano lessons from the terrifying Mrs. Ruth Boyd even though I had no aptitude for it. I was to play "Clair de Lune" at my piano recital, wearing an itchy pink net evening dress.

I was not to like the mountain music that surrounded us on every side, from the men playing banjo and mandolin on the sidewalk outside my daddy's dimestore on Saturdays, to Martha's father playing his guitar down on the riverbank after dinner, to Kitty Wells singing "It Wasn't God Who Made Honky Tonk Angels" on our brand-new radio station, WNRG. But here, my mother ran into serious trouble. For I loved this music. I had been born again to "Angel Band," sung high and sweet at a tent revival that I had to sneak out to go to; and I had a dobro-playing boyfriend, with Nashville aspirations.

Even my mother enjoyed going to the drive-in theater on Saturday evenings in the summer to hear two brothers from over in Dickenson County, Ralph and Carter Stanley, play and sing their bluegrass music on top of the concrete-block concessions stand. "I never will marry, I'll take me no wife; I intend to live single, all of my life," Ralph wailed mournfully, followed by their fast instrumental version of "Shout, Little Lulie." Old people were clogging on the patch of concrete in front of the window where you bought your Cokes and popcorn; little kids were swinging on the iron-pipe swing set. Whole families ate fried chicken and deviled eggs they'd brought from home, sitting on quilts on the grass. My boyfriend reached over and squeezed my sweaty hand. The Stanley Brothers' nasal voices rose higher than the gathering mist, higher than the lightning bugs that rose from the trees along the river as night came on. When it got full dark, the Stanley Brothers climbed down off the concession stand and we all got into our cars and the movie came on.

I loved that music, just as I loved my grandmother's corn pudding and those scary old stories my Uncle Vern told. But this hillbilly music didn't have anything to do with "culture," as I was constantly being reminded. No, "culture" was someplace else, and when the time came, I would be sent off to get some. Culture lived in big cities like Richmond, and Washington, and Boston and New York—especially in New York, especially in places like Carnegie Hall.

Forty years later, I stood on my hundred-dollar balcony seat in Carnegie Hall and screamed as seventy-four-year-old Dr. Ralph Stanley and the rest of the traditional musicians and singers from the phenomenally successful *O Brother, Where Art Thou?* soundtrack played to a sold-out house. Elvis Costello was the emcee; Joel and Ethan Coen, the filmmakers who made the *O Brother* movie, were in the audience, along with T Bone Burnett, its musical director. The Coen Brothers had written this note about the music in the program, aimed at their New York audience: "These songs were for the most part created by people whose lives were hard and horizons narrow. Their lives were not like ours. All that urges their music on us is its humanity . . . And yet, this soundtrack went platinum without receiving any airplay: pop stations considered it too country, and country stations considered it too . . . country."

On stage at Carnegie Hall, the Fairfield Four sang their stark treatment of "Po' Lazarus." Dan Tyminski tore it up on "I Am a Man of Constant Sorrow." The Cox family, fresh from Louisiana, brought down the house with "Will There Be Any Stars in My Crown." Reigning bluegrass princess Alison Krauss fiddled up a storm, then sang "When I Go Down to the River to Pray" in tight harmony with Gillian Welch and Emmylou Harris. They sang so sweet, they could have been angels. The little Peasall sisters—Sarah, age thirteen, Hannah, age ten, and Leah, age eight, wore patent-leather shoes and bows in their hair to sing "In the Highways and the Hedges, I'll Be Somewhere Listening for My Name." Gillian's husband, David Rawlings, teamed up with her on "I Want To Sing That Rock and Roll."

But the night belonged to Ralph Stanley, who came out last, all by himself, and took center stage to give his famous a capella rendition of the terrifying "O Death," with all lights black except for a single spotlight trained directly on him. "O Death, O Death, won't you spare me over for another year?" His high, haunting voice filled the huge dark hall. The song lasted for five minutes, followed by almost a full moment of total silence. Then the stage lights went up, the house lights came on, the other performers rushed out on stage, and the standing ovation went on and on.

Although he loves to poke fun at his own success—recently referring to the movie as "O Brother, Where Art Thou *At*"—Dr. Ralph Stanley has come a long way from the top of the concession stand at the Grundy Drive-In Theater. A six-time Grammy nominee and a Grand Ole Opry member, Stanley was the first recipient of the National Endowment for the Humanities' Traditional American Music Award, and he performed at the inaugurations of both Jimmy Carter and Bill Clinton. He has been awarded the Library of Congress Living Legend Medal.

Dr. Ralph's Carnegie Hall appearance symbolized something that has happened to Appalachian culture as a whole. Now, everybody in the region realizes that we don't have to go anyplace else to "get culture." Every little town has its own little festival, celebrating itself with local music, food, and crafts, whether it's called a "blackberry festival," or a "ramp festival," or a "wooly worm contest," or "gingerbread day," or a "hollering contest," or a "fiddling convention." Fueled by a national, politically-correct appreciation of whatever is still ethnically or geographically or culturally distinct, America as a whole is coming to appreciate and value its differences. Everybody understands that our own Appalachian culture is as rich, and as diverse in terms of history, arts, crafts, literature, folklore, and music, for instance, as any area in this country.

But in fact, we are far richer than most. Our formidable geography acted as a natural barrier for so long, keeping others out, holding us in, allowing for the development of our rich folk culture, our distinctive speech patterns, our strong sense of tradition, and our radical individualism. Appalachian people are more rooted than other Southerners. We still live in big, extended families that spoil children and revere old people. We will talk your ears off. We still excel in storytelling—and I mean everybody, not just some old guy in overalls at a folk festival. I mean the woman who cuts your hair, I mean your doctor, I mean your mother. Our great music is country music—which was always working-class, from its beginnings in the old-time string bands and ballads right up through honky-tonk and the high lonesome sound of bluegrass to present-day glitzy Nashville, and then all the way back around to the current revival of more old-time, traditional music.

Look at Dolly Parton, now a national icon: "I had to get rich to sing this poor," she has said, referring to the success of her albums *The Grass Is Blue*, her take on traditional bluegrass, and *Little Sparrow*, which is old-time, or what Dolly calls her "blue mountain music." Look at Lucinda Williams and Steve Earle and Patty Loveless. And the big national stars just keep on coming, like Kenny Chesney, Florida Georgia Line, Eric Church, and Miranda Lambert . . . country music is mainstream American music now.

But what about our literature? No one could deny that there is a veritable explosion of Appalachian writing today. A lot of it is hitting the best-seller lists, too—this means it is being read, and widely read, outside the region. I'm talking about Charles

Frazier's Civil War novel *Cold Mountain* and Ron Rash's amazing *Serena*, for instance, both set in western North Carolina; about Barbara Kingsolver's *Prodigal Summer*, which takes place near Emory, Virginia; about Sharyn McCrumb's Ballad Novels and Robert Morgan's *Gap Creek*, which even got "Oprah-fied," as did Gwen Hyman Rubio's eastern Kentucky novel *Icy Sparks*. I'm especially talking about Adriana Trigiani's lively comic novels from my own neck of the woods, *Big Stone Gap*, *Big Cherry Holler*, *Milk Glass Moon*.

Big Stone Gap has recently been filmed in Big Stone Gap, Virginia, starring Ashley Judd and directed by Adriana herself. *Cold Mountain* was a hit film even though they shot most of it in Romania, to Charles Frazier's dismay. So was *Walk the Line*, which chronicled the Carter Family and Johnny Cash. *Nashville* is a popular television series. The film *Songcatcher* traced the adventures of a Boston musicologist who comes to visit her crusading sister at a settlement school in Madison County, North Carolina, and sets about "catching"—or transcribing all the local ballads. The darker film *Winter's Bone*, based upon the novel of the same name by Daniel Woodrell and set in Arkansas, deals with the pervasive drug problem in the mountains, as does Ron Rash's *The World Made Straight*.

Newer Appalachian writers such as Silas House, Ann Pancake, and Wiley Cash deal with mountaintop removal mining and other energy and ecological problems besetting the region now. In *Flight Behavior*, Barbara Kingsolver makes it clear that such

Appalachian issues are global issues, too. Widespread Appalachian literature courses, festivals, and writing workshops ought to ensure the fine new crop of young writers—and activists—continues.

Clearly, I could go on and on, and I'm not even really getting into visual arts, or poetry, or design, or drama, or documentary film. My point is that mainstream American culture has become "Appalachian-ized." No matter what you think of NASCAR, for instance—arguably our most successful Appalachian export—it's everyplace now.

I'm of two minds about all this. I was country, remember, when country wasn't cool. I don't really like to see my favorite places and people be "discovered." I'd rather hear Sheila Adams sing a ballad on a mountaintop in Sodom, North Carolina, than on her latest CD. I'd rather eat at Cuz's in Pounding Mill, Virginia, than Cracker Barrel.

Even though I sometimes wish I could be back in the simpler, saner, safer world of my childhood, eating a piece of fried chicken on a quilt at the drive-in theater while Ralph Stanley plays music on top of the concession stand, I know I can't. The drive-in is long gone, and so am I. But I'll tell you something else—I was mighty proud to be there the night Dr. Ralph played at Carnegie Hall.

DIMESTORE

Dimestore

GRUNDY NESTLED IN ITS MOUNTAINS "like a play-pretty cotched in the hand of God," as an old woman once described it. Surely I could always count on these mountains, this river behind our house, this town where I grew up in my father's dimestore and across the street in my grandfather's office at the courthouse and in the Methodist Church and in my grandparents' house just across Slate Creek, right next to my school. "Honey, the only thing you can count on in this world," my granddaddy used to say, "is death and taxes." But that couldn't be true, I felt. This was my geography. It would be like this forever. My daddy knew. He called it his "standing ground."

I could drive that road with my eyes closed, or almost—twisty Route 460 as it wound up through the mountains of southwest Virginia. I turned at Claypool Hill, passed Richlands, and went over the heart-stopping Shortt Gap. I passed the huge Island Creek coal tipple; innumerable "yard sales," held in no yard but right along the roadside; a storefront with a big sign that said WE BUY GINSENG; several houses turned into the kind of freelance churches where you get to scream out and fall down. Like a vision of Hell itself, the coke ovens appeared as I crossed the bridge over the Dismal River, brick chimney after chimney belching red flames into the sky. We used to drive up there and park when I was a teenager—it was the most exciting thing to do on a date (also the only thing, except for the revivals and the movie that changed once a week). There was a lot of traffic as I got closer to Grundy, where the large hollers spill out into the main road: Garden Creek, Big Prater, Little Prater, Watkins Branch, and Hoot Owl Holler, just beyond the house I grew up in. Somebody was sure to greet me by rolling down the window of his truck and yelling, "Hi, Lee, when did you get in?"

I was always struck by that preposition *in*. Driving into Grundy was like heading into a bowl, producing that familiar sense of enclosure that used to comfort me and drive me wild all at the same time when I was a teenager. These mountains are so steep that the sun seemed to set about 3 p.m., so steep that a cow once fell off a cliff straight down through the roof and landed in my Aunt Bess and Uncle Clyde's kitchen in downtown Grundy, close to the courthouse. This is true.

Founded at the confluence of the Levisa Fork River and Slate

Creek, Grundy became the county seat of Buchanan County in 1858, enduring cycles of fire and flood, bust and boom, as lumber and coal businesses came and went. Perhaps its isolation and its constant struggles were what made its citizens so close to each other, so caring and generous—"the best people in the world," my daddy always said, and this is true, too. Even after Mama died, I could never get him to retire and leave Grundy.

"No, honey, I need me a mountain to rest my eyes against," Daddy always said.

MY VERY FIRST MEMORY IS of downtown Grundy. I'm standing up in my crib, gripping its spool railings, looking out an upstairs dormer window of my grandparents' house at the flickering colored lights of the Morgan Theater, reflected in the waters of Slate Creek. First green, then yellow, then blue and red and green again, they twinkle through the distance like fairy lights in an enchanted kingdom, promising everything. In my mind's eye, I can see them still, mysterious, beautiful, and always too far away. I've been told I watched them steadily for hours, and it must be so, for that memory is indelible, as is the somber striking of the courthouse clock that marked the passing of every hour.

It is 1945. I am one year old. My father, Ernest Smith, is away in the Navy. My mother, Virginia Marshall Smith (nicknamed "Gig"), has left her job teaching home economics at the high school and is working at the Ration Board. She and I are living with my grandparents until my daddy returns. Then we will move into our own house up the river at Cowtown and Daddy will open the Five and Ten Cent Variety Store with the financial help of his uncle Curt Smith (who was actually Daddy's own age—it was that kind of family). Though the store will later become a Ben Franklin, it would always be known in town as simply "the dimestore."

Many of my favorite memories of Grundy take place in this dimestore. As a little girl, my job was "taking care of the dolls." Not only did I comb their hair and fluff up their frocks, but I also made up long, complicated life stories for them, things that had happened to them before they came to the dimestore, things that would happen to them after they left my care. I gave each of them three-part names: Mary Elizabeth Satterfield, for instance, and Baby Betsy Black. Their lives were very dramatic.

Upstairs in my father's office, I got to type on a typewriter, count money, and talk to Roberta Ratliff, pale, blonde, and pretty as a princess in a fairy-tale book. She would later become the manager. I spent hours and hours upstairs in that office, observing the whole floor of the dimestore through the one-way glass window and reveling in my own power—nobody can see me, but I can see everybody! I witnessed not only shoplifting, but fights and embraces as well. Thus I learned the position of the omniscient narrator, who sees and records everything, yet is never visible. It was the perfect early education for a fiction writer.

I always went down to check on the goldfish in their basement tank. And every spring I looked forward to the arrival of the pastel-colored Easter chickens. But my favorites were the little round turtles with roses painted on their shells. I used to wear these turtles to school on my sweaters, where they clung like brooches. I liked to visit with John Yuhasz, a very kind man, on my trips to the basement to "help" him put up stock. Clovis Owens, in charge of maintenance, could fix anything, and his wife made the best pound cake in the world. She always sent me a piece, wrapped in wax paper.

Up on the main floor, I chatted with the dimestore "girls" who had all been working there for as long as I could remember— sweet Ellen Clevinger in children's wear; Viola, back in piece goods, who always hugged me; floor supervisor Ruth Edwards; and Ruby Sweeton, supposedly in toiletries, who seemed to be everywhere. With bright red spots of rouge on her cheeks, Mildred Shortridge presided over the popcorn machine and the candy counter at the front of the store, whispering the craziest things in my ear. She made me laugh and laugh. I always bought some of the jellied orange slices and the nonpareils, those flat chocolate discs covered with hard little white balls of sugar. My friends were surprised to find that I never got anything free at the dimestore; despite my protests, I had to save my allowance and pay just like everybody else.

• • •

I WAS ALLOWED TO RUN free all over town, which was filled with our relatives, not only Smiths, but Dennises and Belchers as well. Russell Belcher ran the Rexall drugstore. Uncle Curt Smith owned the Lynwood Theater and lived with his wife Lyde and her sister Nora Belcher in a shotgun apartment above it, reached by a long, dark staircase. I was fascinated by this apartment, where the rooms were all in a row and Lyde cooked a big hot lunch in the middle of every day. Uncle Vern Smith (longtime member of the Virginia State Legislature) and his son Harold had opened the first Ford Agency. Uncle Clyde Dennis ran the insurance agency. Uncle Percy Dennis, Sr., was the Superintendent of Schools, while Percy Dennis, Jr., operated the Mingo lumber yard across the river. My grandfather's alcoholic brother, piano-playing Blind Bill Smith, often came over from West Virginia to play boogie-woogie piano for dances. My grandparents Chloe and Earl Smith lived across Slate Creek from town in a big old brick house reached by a scary swinging bridge that I crossed each time with my heart in my mouth.

I went to town every single day when school let out, across that swinging bridge and then the real bridge they built later on. First I went to the dimestore and got some candy from Mildred and did my homework upstairs in the office, or crossed the street to the old stone courthouse and did my homework in my grandaddy's treasurer's office, eavesdropping all the while. In the dimestore I learned who was pregnant, who was getting married, who had got saved, who had got churched for drinking, who was mean to her children or made the best red velvet cake. In the courthouse I'd hear a different kind of story—who was in jail, who had gone bankrupt or shot his brother or tried to short his employees, who was out of a job or had set his house on fire just to collect the insurance money. I also liked to go around the county politicking with Granddaddy on Sunday afternoons, sitting down to eat some Sunday dinner with everybody. I liked to stand out on the courthouse corner with him on Saturdays when he gave out dollar bills. Men would be smoking and shooting dice and "loafering around telling lies," as Grandaddy said, on the courthouse bench, and boys would be shining shoes. Somebody would always be playing music, guitar and fiddle and maybe banjo, out on the sidewalk in front of the dimestore.

Next to the dimestore was the Rexall drugstore, where as a teenager I gossiped with my girlfriends, bought Maybelline makeup, ate mysterious "meat sandwiches," and read *Teen* magazine with its articles like "How to Talk to Boys (Tip: Learn about Cars)." Then came Russell's Men's Store where I held Christmas jobs during high school; and finally, Uncle Curt's Lynwood Theater which I attended virtually every time the movie changed during my entire life in Grundy.

Here, for the cost of a mere quarter, the big silver screen brought us the rest of the world. Here we formed our notions of bravery, of glamour, of danger and sophistication, of faraway places and people like no people we had ever seen. Western theme music swelled our hearts. Our ideal of heroism came from stoic John Wayne; of beauty, from Jane Russell and Marilyn Monroe. Was anything ever as scary as *Hush . . . Hush, Sweet Charlotte*? Or as sad as *Imitation of Life*? We found Ma and Pa Kettle hilarious, and howled at the Three Stooges, the Marx Brothers, and later, Jerry Lewis. Our first dates took place at the Lynwood ("Nice girls do not sit in the balcony!" our mothers decreed) where we grimly held our dates' hands in a kind of death grip throughout the whole show, afraid we'd hurt their feelings if we stopped for even one minute to wipe off our sweaty palms.

The movies taught me that place can be almost as important as personality, and that actions really do speak louder than words. Plot is all-important; beginning, middle, and end is the most natural and satisfying sequence of events. Most important of all: something has to happen. People in a movie do not just sit around thinking all the time, the way I did in real life—"mooning around," my mother called it, disgustedly.

From Main Street, it was only a stone's throw to our little Methodist Church. With its chiseled stone exterior and beautiful stained-glass windows, it looked totally different from every other church in town—much more holy, I felt! Its slightly damp, mildewy smell was a holy smell, too. At Christmas, each child received a paper bag containing an orange, an apple, some walnuts, and a Hershey bar. In the Christmas pageant, I was first an animal, then a wise man, and finally an angel, but never the Virgin Mary. The Virgin Mary could not have curly hair. On Mother's Day, you wore a red carnation corsage to church if your mother was still alive and a white carnation if your mother was dead, something I could not imagine. Everybody wore a corsage on Easter Sunday. Summer's Vacation Bible School featured Lorna Doone cookies and red Kool-Aid in paper cups. We made lanyards and sang, "Red and yellow, black and white, they are precious in his sight, Jesus loves the little children of the world," though we had never seen any of those other ones. Later, at Youth Fellowship, we made pizza, which we called "pizza pie." We had learned about it on our summer trip to Myrtle Beach. "Ju-ust as I a-am, without one plea," we sang tremulously at revivals, where I always rededicated my life, to my mother's embarrassment. "A nice girl does not rededicate her life at the drop of a hat," she said. We ate three-bean salad and coconut cake at church suppers.

From church we crossed Slate Creek on the swinging bridge to my grandparents' house. A low stone wall separated their front yard from the road in front of it. I remember the paw-paw trees by the gate, the pungent smell of the pods rotting on the ground. I remember looking up from the yard to watch a long, slow line of people carrying a casket up Hibbetts Hill for burial in the town cemetery. "Oh where is my dear brother? Oh where is my dear sister? Day is a-breaking in my soul," they sang.

My grandmother's flower garden, to the right as you faced

the porch, was her pride and joy, perhaps the purest expression of herself—for she had an innate artistic bent, a love of beauty and poetry, that had nothing to do with her own biography: an isolated childhood up on Fletchers Ridge, marriage at sixteen, and a lack of formal education. But she never stopped learning. In her later years, she attended summer courses at Lake Junaluska, the Methodist version of Chautauqua. Their house was filled with books and catalogs that she had sent off for. She sent off for some of her plants, too, which bloomed in astonishing variety and profusion. Her garden was like an English garden, its flowers planted in clusters rather than rows. A clematis-covered white lattice arch shaded two benches and a table. In curlicue lettering, an iron placard proclaimed:

The kiss of the sun for pardon,
The song of the birds for mirth,
I am nearer God's heart in a garden
Than anywhere else on earth.

The living room was too dark and too formal for me as a child, with its flowered carpet, velvet armchairs with fancy lace antimacassars on their backs and armrests, the hissing radiator behind them, and the piecrust table with its tiers of dainty knickknacks that I was just dying to break, particularly that white china lady from Japan. My grandmother would sit in a wine velvet wingchair, all dressed up in some kind of filmy voile dress with matching brooch and earrings. She seemed to have hundreds of these sets. When she died, I was astonished to learn that they were all fake. Grandmother—for this is what we were instructed to call her at all times—received a steady stream of visitors. Years later, I learned that my own mother had first developed serious colitis "about the time I realized that I was expected to visit your grandmother every day."

Still, Mama and my Aunt Lois often brought me and my cousins Randy and Melissa over there in the summertime: in my memory, the mothers are always sitting on the porch sewing or stringing beans, watching to see who'll come up the road or stop in for a glass of iced tea. We loved the big swing and the comfortable wicker furniture. The whole family came over on Sunday afternoons. Most of the men were in politics, yellow-dog Democrats always running somebody for office or politicking and agitating about something. They were all big talkers. They'd drink some whiskey out behind the house and after a while they would bet good money on just about anything, even which bird would fly first off the telephone wire, and then everybody would stay out on the porch talking and telling stories until it got dark and we could all see the fairy lights of the Morgan Theater's marquee over in town. I usually fell asleep on somebody's lap, looking at those lights and hearing those stories, told by somebody that loved me, so that my sense of a story is still very personal. Even today, when I'm writing, stories usually come to me in a human voice; often it is the voice of a character, but sometimes it is the voice of the story itself.

My sweet granddaddy, a kind man with a Humpty Dumpty figure in later years, always wore a suit and a hat to town. He loved children, often serving as ringmaster for our circuses in the yard. He also loved the Cincinnati Reds, listening avidly to their games on his giant Philco radio upstairs in the bedroom by the side window.

Grandmother, too, spent many hours before her own side window right below, sitting on the blue tufted sofa with all those little covered buttons. The view from their respective windows symbolized the changes that were taking place in Grundy: originally, my grandparents looked out upon their own vegetable garden, the barn and various outbuildings, the chickens and the cow, the woods and the mountains. Later they could see the narrow-gauge railroad headed for West Virginia, and the growing town just down at the mouth of Slate. In their final years, this view was cut off by the first modern supermarket in Grundy, Jack Smith's Piggly Wiggly, which he built right next to my grandparents' house on the biggest piece of unoccupied flat land in the downtown area, where land was suddenly at a premium. "Progress" triumphs over nature every time, and Grundy was no exception. The late sixties and early seventies were boom times for coal and expansion years for business in Grundy. In those years, of course, nobody even considered the effects of unregulated growth upon the environment.

I went to school right on the other side of my grandparents' house, in the stately old school building that is now the

Appalachian School of Law. Here I encountered the terrifying Miss Nellie Hart, with her bright white hair, foghorn voice, and beautiful skin, who could diagram any sentence, even sentences so complex that their diagrams on the board looked like blueprints for a cathedral. It was an ability I aspired to. I loved English, flunked math, and admired my gorgeous and sophisticated French teacher, Anita Cummings, who wore her hair appropriately in a French twist, and gave us quiche lorraine to eat in class. Astonishingly, she was married to the football coach. I liked funny Mrs. Garber, in whose class I made a spectacularly ugly yellow blouse with darts that went the wrong way. I approached my job as football cheerleader with utmost seriousness, practicing endlessly at home, though I never knew the first thing about the game. I could do a cartwheel and land in a split, however. I remember the yellow-tiled cafeteria where I surreptitiously picked up all the Peppermint Pattie wrappers ever touched by the football player I had a crush on, then saved them at home in little silver stacks in my dresser drawer. My girlfriends and I decorated that cafeteria with endless rolls of crepe paper for dances where I slow-danced with the Peppermint Pattie boy to "The Twelfth of Never," our song.

I remember the auditorium where study hall was held and where to everyone's shock I was once crowned Miss Grundy High in spite of my amazingly awful outfit: a red velvet ribbon tied around my neck like a noose; a white strapless dress with about two hundred rows of tacky little net ruffles marching all the way down its ballerina-length hoop skirt to my red high heels. This outfit was my own concept entirely. I won a rhinestone tiara, a glittery banner proclaiming MISS GRUNDY HIGH, an armful of real red roses, a steam iron, and a set of white Samsonite luggage, which my cousins had to lug home because my date wouldn't give me a ride. Now, he said, I'd "get too stuck up." I cried all the way home. My parents were out playing bridge with the Beinhorns, and missed the whole thing. "A nice girl should not win a beauty contest" was my mother's opinion.

When I think of Mama, she is always at home, holding forth in her kitchen, and somebody is always there visiting. Most often it's Ava McClanahan, who helped her for years, or one of her many friends or neighbors: Stella Burke, Margaret Pritchard, June Bevins, or Dot Trivett, for instance. The kitchen is filled with cigarette smoke, the smell of coffee perking, and whatever's baking in the oven; often it is Mama's famous loaf bread. The women lean forward, over their coffee cups, and lower their voices. Writing or drawing at my own little table in the corner, I perk right up. Now they are going to *really* talk, about somebody who "has just never been quite right, bless her heart," or somebody who is "kindly nervous," or somebody else who's "been having trouble down there." *Down there* is a secret place, a foreign country, like Mexico or Nicaragua. I keep on drawing, and don't miss a word. Mama takes the loaf bread out of the oven and gives us all a piece, crusty on the outside and soft on the inside, with butter melting into it. It is the best thing in the world. Country music plays softly on the countertop radio, tuned to our brand-new station, WNRG; in my mind it's always Johnny Cash, singing "Ring of Fire." The Levisa River flows out back, with the railroad on the other side, carrying Norfolk & Western trains loaded with coal.

How I loved the mournful whistle of those trains as they roared past several times a day! Often I ran out and stood there on the riverbank watching them pass, wondering where they were going. On the edge of the riverbank sat the little "writing house" that my daddy built for me and then had to build back again after every flood.

My mother had been raised at Chincoteague Island, on Virginia's far Eastern Shore; she had just graduated from Madison State Teachers College when she met my father at a family wedding; her older sister, Marion, married his uncle John Dennis, creating some kind of complicated cousins I never could figure out. As a girl, Mama was beautiful and light-hearted—silly, even. She loved to dance. Daddy fell hard. With both the time and the inclination for courting, he would not be put off, arriving in Chincoteague ten days later, only to learn that she had to leave immediately for Harrisburg, Pennsylvania, her first teaching job. She'd scarcely been there a week when—to her surprise—Ernest Smith showed up. He took a room at a local boardinghouse near her own rented quarters, then appeared bright and early each morning to drive her to school, and at the end of every school day, he'd be waiting by the gate with a bunch of roadside flowers and a big grin on his face. This went on for months. The whole town took a fancy to it. By Thanksgiving, he had worn her down; at Christmas vacation, they eloped.

Thus Mama came to Grundy, where she taught home economics, quitting after many years to "raise me." When I was little, she read aloud to me constantly; I believe it is for this reason that I came to love reading so much, for I always heard her voice in my head as I read the words on the page. She never got used to the lack of a horizontal horizon or the fact that the sun couldn't reach our yard before 11 a.m., not enough sun to really grow roses, though her roses looked okay to me. Still, she loved Grundy almost as much as Daddy did, despite the floods that twice destroyed her house and yard. They built it all back each time. My mother loved that house, as she loved her roses and her crafts. My own North Carolina home today is filled with quilts and afghans she made, furniture she refinished, and pictures she decoupaged. "Hell, Gig will decoupage anything—she'll decoupage a chair while you're sitting on it!" neighbor Dr. Burkes was heard to say.

COWTOWN WAS A WONDERFUL neighborhood to grow up in, roaming from house to house with our gang of neighborhood kids—my best friend Martha Sue Owens, Melissa and Randy and other visiting cousins, Rowena and Bill Yates, Cathy and Russ Belcher, Jimmy Bevins and little Terry Trivett, the Boxley boys who came to stay with their grandmother in the summertime. I ate supper at all their houses. Gaynor Owens made the best cream gravy and cornbread, but the Trivetts ate the most exotic things, even foreign things, such as lasagna and chop suey. I learned to swim in their backyard pool.

Martha Sue and I started a neighborhood newspaper named *The Small Review*, which we wrote out laboriously by hand and sold door to door for a nickel. I got in lots of trouble for my editorials, such as "George McGuire Is Too Grumpy," or my opinion that "Mrs. Ruth Boyd is a mean music teacher. She hits your fingers with a pencil and her house smells like meat loaf all the time." We also wrote news items such as the following: "Miss Lee Smith and Miss Martha Sue Owens were taken by car to Bristol, Virginia, to buy school shoes. They got to look at their feet in a machine at Buster Brown and guess what. Their bones are LONG AND GREEN."

We kids formed dozens of clubs, each with its secret handshake and code words. We ran our mountains ridge to ridge—climbing trees and cliffs, playing in caves, swinging on grapevines, catching salamanders, damming up creeks, building lean-tos and lookouts, playing Indians and settlers with our handmade slingshots or the occasional Christmas bow-and-arrow set. Every day after school we'd throw down our books and "head for the hills." We'd stay there until they rang the bell to call us home for supper.

Back in my own yard, I spent a lot of time sitting under a giant cluster of forsythia bushes, which I called the "dogbushes" because I took an endless series of family dogs under there with me—my Pekingese, Misty, and our boxer, Queenie, come to mind—along with an entire town full of imaginary friends. My two best friends in that dogbush town were Sylvia and Vienna (who was named for my favorite food, the Vienna sausages in the nice flat little cans that I used to take under there with me to eat, along with some of those little cellophane packets of saltine crackers). My friend Vienna was very beautiful, with long, red curly hair. But my friend Sylvia could fly. I also spent hours down by the river, where I had a wading house—the understory of a willow tree—which would find its way into my first novel, *The Last Day the Dogbushes Bloomed*.

I wasn't allowed to play in the Levisa when it ran black with the coal they were washing upriver. But once Martha Sue and I made rafts out of boards tied on to inner tubes and floated down past the Richardson Apartments and under the Hoot Owl Bridge, around the bend at the hospital and under the depot bridge, all the way to town, where we landed in triumph behind the dimestore. Here we were greeted by a sizable crowd including my daddy, alerted by enemy spies. We were quickly returned, dripping wet, to our worried mothers for a spanking.

THE LEVISA SEEMED SO TAME then. Impossible to imagine that this friendly stream could become a raging torrent as it had done in 1937 and then again in the great flood of 1957, when I found a huge catfish flopping down the dimestore stairs into the water-filled toy section. My little dead turtles were floating everywhere, with roses on their shells. After it flooded again in 1977, I came home to help. I remember gathering up floating pieces of the parquet floor in my mother's dining room to keep as building blocks for my little boys back in North Carolina. The muddy water had risen above the countertops in Mama's kitchen. That flood killed three people, devastated 90 percent of the downtown businesses, and caused $100 million in damage countywide. Those were the "twenty-year floods," but there were other floods, too—Grundy had had nine major floods since 1929. Daddy never slept when it rained. He was always out back with his flashlight, "checking the river." He had an enormous steel flood door constructed for the back of the dimestore, which was put into place each time the river started rising.

Daddy finally closed his dimestore in 1992 due to lack of business, despite everyone's pleas that he keep it open. I thought he should, too. Since my mother's death four years earlier, I couldn't imagine what he would do when the dimestore was gone. Its popular lunch counter had made it not only a store but also a gathering place, a landmark. But Daddy was too good a businessman to "run a losing proposition," as he put it. The town population had been declining for years due to the floods and the failing coal industry. There had been 35,000 people in Buchanan County when I was growing up there; the population had fallen to around 28,000. Three thousand people had lived in Grundy alone during the coal boom days of the early 1970s; now there were fewer than a thousand. Unemployment had soared to 16 percent.

Watching my father close his dimestore after forty-seven years in business was one of the saddest things I have ever witnessed; in a way it was fitting that he died on the last day of his going-out-of-business sale. He was eighty-two.

I had been visiting him for a week. Everybody we ever knew had come by the store to pay their respects and buy something, one last thing from the dimestore. All the merchandise had been sold, and some men had come from Bluefield to take away the fixtures, which had been sold, too. They loaded their big truck and drove off. Daddy and I walked out of the store together; he turned off the light and locked the door behind us. I headed back down to my home in North Carolina, and Daddy went back to his house in Cowtown, where he ate the supper which one of the girls had sent home with him, read the paper and the mail, and at some point fell to the kitchen floor, breaking several ribs.

He lay there all night, until Ava McClanahan came by to check on him and fix him some breakfast the next morning.

I was back in North Carolina, getting ready for school, when the hospital called. My father was okay, the doctor told me, but they were going to keep him until I got there. I canceled my class, jumped back in the car, and drove that road I knew by heart. I was already planning to bring him back to North Carolina with me for a while, willing or not.

I found Daddy sitting up in bed, ready to go home as soon as they would let him. "I tell you what," he said, handing me a $50 bill. "These nurses have been so sweet to me, I want you to go over to the Piggly Wiggly right now and buy them some candy, about six boxes. Buy some real good candy, like Whitman's Samplers. Go on right now, they're fixing to close." Behind him, one of those nurses smiled indulgently, shaking her head. Everybody knew what Ernest Smith was like. And I knew better than to argue.

I came back with the candy to a very different scene, the hospital room suddenly filled with frantically busy people, Daddy's bed surrounded, the doctor running down the hall toward us, his white coat flying out behind him. "Code Blue in Room 112, Code Blue in Room 112," the loudspeaker kept repeating. "Hit's a hemhorrhage, honey," a nurse said, pulling me back, "from his stomach. Why don't you just stay out here with me." I knew this nurse from high school.

After that, things happened very fast.

• • •

AND THEN VERY SLOWLY, AS Grundy turned into a ghost town. An ambitious plan for flood-proofing the town was said to be in the works, but it was a long time coming. One by one the old stores closed. New businesses would not move into the empty buildings of the flood plain; they became increasingly dilapidated. We gave the dimestore to the community, which used it as a much-needed teen center—one of the few down-town buildings in use at all. Traffic slowed, then nearly ceased. Parking places stood empty. The last car dealership closed. With the coal business in decline, Grundy was being kept alive mostly because it was the county seat; government continued in the old stone courthouse across the street.

The new Appalachian School of Law, which opened its doors in 1995, had brought some much-needed new energy and ideas to town despite the fact that it was very difficult for faculty or students to find housing, meals, or merchandise in Grundy—both of the closest towns, Richlands, Virginia, and Pikeville, Kentucky, were at least forty-five minutes away.

I DROVE THAT TWISTY ROAD again when I went to say good-bye to old Grundy in 2005, a few weeks before they would blow up the dimestore, which I found already boarded up. I got out my camera and took a picture of it. The dimestore would be demolished along with three dozen other Main Street stores and a score of homes as part of the drastic and daring $177 million

Grundy Flood Control and Redevelopment Project, which was finally under way, a historic collaboration among the U.S. Army Corps of Engineers, the Virginia State Department of Transportation, and the Town of Grundy itself, population by then 1,100. They planned to move the railroad and rebuild U.S. 460 on top of a fourteen-foot levee running where the buildings once stood.

"New Grundy" would rise on the newly created moonscape I stood looking at across the deceptively docile Levisa River: thirteen astonishingly flat acres where a mountain had once stood until very recently, when they had blasted away 2.3 million cubic yards of it. The idealistic concept of "raising Grundy" reminded me of that old gospel song, "Lord lift me up and let me stand, by faith on Heaven's table land . . ." Now a 300-foot wall of rock rose straight up behind the flat area, Heaven's table land. I took several pictures of the site. New bridges would connect the "new town" with the older Walnut Street and historic courthouse area, I was told.

"Doesn't it make you sad?" friends asked.

Well, yes and no.

Of course I felt sentimental and nostalgic, but then I hadn't been driving 35 miles one way to buy a shower curtain. And I'm a merchant's daughter, remember. Unfailingly civic, Daddy always loved Grundy, and I knew he would have supported any plan to save it.

But . . . *Walmart?*

Grundy may be one of the only towns in the United States that has ever actually invited Walmart into its downtown area, instead of organizing against it. The moonscape's new "retail center" would be anchored by a unique Walmart Supercenter sitting on the third floor of a 500-space parking building. Shoppers would take their carts up and down on a giant escalator. A three-story Walmart with a giant escalator! Looking at those muddy acres, it sounded like science fiction to me.

The town fathers had made this unilateral decision themselves; no public referendum or vote was ever held. Though some local opponents formed a group called People Allied for Grundy, led by lawyer Mickey McGlothlin, they didn't get anywhere. Some merchants simply pocketed their government payouts and closed forever. Some had already moved out of town. Others were moving up the hollers or into a metal-shell building up the road, known as the Grundy Mall. The town offices and *The Virginia Mountaineer* newspaper were already there, along with Elaine's Boutique and the Street Law Firm. Terry's Tobacco had gone online.

"We had to look at it for the betterment of all the people," Town Manager Chuck Crabtree told me earnestly at the time. "We had to think, how do you bring the people in? We want to reenergize the town and bring the people back. We want to give them a revitalized town to come to, a place to stop and shop. It's not Walmart that kills your town, it's the location of Walmart. So we're bringing it downtown. Our tax base will skyrocket. It'll be the best thing that's ever happened to this community. I have staked my whole life and my reputation on this."

I took a few more pictures of the empty main street and all the boarded-up stores before I left. I was glad my father had not seen this. He never wanted to retire or leave Grundy, and I could not imagine how he would have spent his days when his beloved dimestore was gone.

Now, I realized, his kind of business could be gone forever.

MAY 2012: I HAVEN'T BEEN back home in a couple of years. For one thing, I don't have any relatives living here now; I go to Abingdon to visit most of them. But today I'm heading up that twisty Route 460 toward Grundy where I will present a program commemorating the fiftienth anniversary of the Buchanan County Public Library; my mother was on its founding board. And also—I have to admit—I am very curious to take a look at that three-story Walmart, which has just opened (finally!) with much fanfare.

The muddy moonscape with its forlorn little sign reading WALMART COMING SOON stood empty for so many years that many people ceased believing in it altogether. Instead of Walmart, the recession came, then deepened. Funding slowed down. Everything stalled. That optimistic town manager disappeared. A huge boulder rolled down off a mountaintop to crush the area's one remaining movie theater, so—outside of school activities—there'd been absolutely nothing for teenagers to do. They couldn't even make out up at the coke ovens—they'd closed, too. An entire generation of children had grown up in the town of Grundy, which was no town at all—there was simply nothing there.

But this is a gorgeous Appalachian spring day, with redbud and sarvis and dogwood blooming on the pale green mountainsides and a deep blue sky arching overhead. Speaking of those mountainsides, they look different, I suddenly realize as I drive along. The Beatrice mine tower is gone, along with the other old tipples and trolleys. I remember the slag heaps often smoking near the tops of the mountains, and the little frame houses clustered on the steep slopes below—where are they? And what about the old company towns, gone too? Where is Raven? I wonder as I leave Richlands. Where is Red Jacket? And what was the name of that big company town with the large houses over in the bottom by the river? Deel! What has happened to Deel? To Vansant? All the outlying communities seem to have disappeared as I approach Grundy. Signs read WE BUY GOLD AND SILVER now, instead of WE BUY GINSENG. Sleek metal coal trucks have replaced the old self-owned and decorated trucks with personal signs like DON'T LAUGH, IT'S PAID FOR and names like "Tennessee Stud." The coal company offices have disappeared or been turned into "energy" companies, i.e., gas, with Consol Energy predominating. I note several locations. The coke ovens are burning again, but now run by SUNCOKE ENERGY, JEWELL OPERATIONS, a sign proclaims. The former bowling alley is a well-drilling business. Big pipes for pipelines lie in stacks everywhere. At Oakwood, the old Garden High School has become the new Appalachian College of Pharmacy, and there's the impressive Twin Valley Middle School, too.

The closer I get to Grundy, the heavier the traffic is; we crawl along bumper to bumper on the newly widened and raised Rt. 460, which is still under construction. Huge machines lift red dirt and rocks into huge trucks; dust fills the air. My old neighborhood, Cowtown, looks totally shocking. Only my own house has not been raised up to the level of the new highway (it can't be, I later learn, due to its frame construction). It looks fragile and dingy, so much older and smaller and lower than the other houses, each of them sitting up on its own divot of earth, like toy houses set up on stands for display. At the end of the driveway behind "my" house, I catch sight of the last incarnation of my writing house, poised on the riverbank with a glint of the river behind. The mountainside across 460 where we used to run so wild and free has been sheared off, a red wound with rock at the top.

Finally the traffic crawls around the bend of the Levisa to Hoot Owl Holler, filled with personal meaning for me as the setting for my novel *Oral History*. A new green road sign reading

POPLAR GAP PARK, FOURTEEN MILES points across the Levisa River Bridge and up the mountain, where a large mesa created by mountaintop removal mining has now—in a brilliant stroke of public relations—been turned into a public park. It boasts picnic facilities, athletic fields, playgrounds, tennis courts, and the state-of-the-art Consol Energy Stage for large events such as concerts. Sunsets viewed from atop Poplar Gap are said to be spectacular. Operated by the county, the park was much needed and is heavily used for everything from the "Race for the Cure Relay" to fireworks and horse shows. I have been reading about it in *The Virginia Mountaineer*, to which I have always subscribed.

Slowly I pass the attractive Comfort Inn at the bend of the river, a new Italian restaurant, and the 24-hour Waffle Shop. I don't check into the Comfort Inn yet, afraid that with all this traffic, I won't have time to see "the new Grundy" before my program begins at the library. There's only the one road, route 460, to get anyplace. Finally the traffic inches down the hill and Walmart comes into view, a behemoth on its big flat lot. It is enormous! Any letter on its sign WALMART is taller than any of the tractor-trailer trucks bringing it merchandise. It looks more like a huge alien spacecraft than like a building. Traffic flows across its bridges, a steady stream in and out of it, back and forth from town, which is still a construction site, though the existing stores and buildings on Maple Street and the court-house area are busy. The sidewalks are thronged with people, all kinds of people! I don't see one single person that I know. Finally I find a parking place in the public lot where the old stone Methodist Church once stood. I have to grin as I remember our singing "red and yellow, black and white, they are precious in his sight"—Grundy actually has some diversity now.

"There's not another town in the nation that has undergone this much change this fast," my friend Debbie Raines, still the senior high school English teacher, has told me. "It is a totally unique situation. You're still here, but your town is gone . . . and when you go to the grocery store now, you see all these strangers," referring not only to the folks who have come in with Walmart but to the influx of new people who have moved in with the Appalachian School of Law and the University of Appalachia's School of Pharmacy. A new optometry school is planned. Whoever would have thought of Grundy as a college town? The college students are involved in community service projects everywhere, from teaching kids soccer to weatherproofing houses. Newcomers are scrambling to find anyplace at all to live; apartments are going up all over the place. "Psychologically, it's hard to undergo this much change," Debbie said. "So many different ideas are being brought into this community, our whole small-town value system is changing. It's very threatening to our older, more conservative residents. It makes it easier to leave here now."

But I have to admit, I enjoy the latte I buy at the new coffee shop, Perks, which has opened up in my Aunt Bess and Uncle

Clyde's old house—that same house where the cow fell through the roof. I take a picture of this coffee shop, to send to my cousin Randy in Denver.

I have to hurry in order to make my program. I find myself gritting my teeth as I cross the Levisa and follow the signs into the mammoth three-story Walmart which looks even bigger, if possible, close up. Its scale is more suited to Charlotte, or New York. I am directed up to the second parking level, which is nearly full. I park and just sit in the car for a minute, not sure whether I can do this or not.

Finally I get out and walk over to ride the giant up escalator, astonished by the people with full carts riding the down escalator. I couldn't even image how this would work, yet it works fine.

There's an open area at the top with a huge picture window and a panoramic view of the town. I don't even get a good look before I am greeted by the Greeter, a large, friendly older fellow named Charles Clevinger, with local ties, as evidenced by his accent and his name. Whoever picked him out knew what they were doing. His father grew up here, and he spent summers here with his grandparents. He asks me if I remember the Rexall and the dimestore. Charles Clevinger refers to Walmart complex as the "Grundy Town Center," proudly enumerating the other stores that are already open on the ground floor: Unique Nails; a sporting goods store; Subway; GameStop; and Factory Connection, a clothing store. Not a single one is local;

not a single one has moved over from "old Grundy." I hadn't even noticed a smaller two-story building under construction at Walmart's base; Clevinger points it out and tells me that it will house a beauty college and salon, plus several offices, with a coal company on top. A free-standing Taco Bell will occupy a grassy plot behind. Another spot is being saved for a "sit-down, fine-dining" restaurant, such as Applebee's (though actually the town fathers just ran Applebee's off because they serve mixed drinks.)

I'm thinking I could use a mixed drink myself, or several. Maybe I'll buy some wine.

I ask where it is and then start up a brightly lit, well-stocked aisle in the grocery section, with its bins of specials in the middle—exactly like every aisle in every Walmart in the world. But before I get to the wine I run into some former Cowtown neighbors who have already got their cart all loaded up. "Oh hey, Lee," she says, "When did you get in?" and continues without missing a beat, "Isn't this Walmart just wonderful? I tell you, it has changed our lives." Her husband stands grinning behind her.

I manage to nod but turn on my heel without a word. No I can't do this, I realize. I cannot. I rush back out to the open escalator area where smiling Charles Clevinger has latched onto some other visitor, thank God, so that I have a chance to walk over to the huge wraparound picture window and get a good look at Grundy from this high vantage point: there's the flat moonscape area below us, crisscrossed by its tiny access roads with their tiny colorful cars; the busy bridges; the tame little river that started it all, improbably, running between its high ringwalls; route 460, where the old stores used to be. Across the eternal traffic jam, I can see Maple Street, the post office, the Appalachian School of Law, the Masonic Lodge—everything up to the bend of Slate Creek. The old stone courthouse with its high clock tower, once the largest and handsomest building in the county, has shrunk to insignificance. I take another picture. Later, I will blow it up. Viewed from the top floor of Walmart, the entire town looks like a toy town, like the train set Daddy always kept set up in the dimestore's basement toy section.

SUDDENLY I REMEMBER A long-ago spring in Grundy, one Sunday afternoon several weeks before Easter. Daddy had taken me down to the dimestore with him to help make the Easter baskets, which didn't come premade and packaged in those days. Many of the girls who worked in the store were there, too, and lots of little chocolate rabbits, and lots of candy Easter eggs. The women formed into an informal assembly line, laughing and gossiping among themselves. They were drinking coffee, wearing slacks and tennis shoes. It was almost a party atmosphere. As a "helper," I didn't last long. I stuffed myself with marshmallow chickens and then crawled into a big box of cellophane straw, where I promptly fell asleep while the straw shifted and settled around me, eventually covering me entirely, so nobody could find me when it was time to go.

"Lee!" I heard my daddy calling. "Lee!" The overhead fluorescent lights in the dimestore glowed down pink through the cellophane straw. It was the most beautiful thing I have ever seen. "Lee!" they called. I knew I'd have to answer soon, but I held that moment as long as I could, safe and secure in that bright pink world, listening to my father call my name.

Recipe Box

MY MOTHER'S RECIPE BOX SITS on the windowsill in our North Carolina kitchen where my eye falls on it twenty, maybe thirty times a day. I will never move it. An anachronism in my own modern kitchen, the battered box contains my mother's whole life story, in a way, with all its places and phases, all her hopes and the accommodations she made in the name of love, as I have done, as we all do. I can read it like a novel—for in fact, our recipes tell us everything about us: where we live, what we value, how we spend our time. Mama's recipe box is an odd green-gold in color. She "antiqued" it, then decoupaged it with domestic decals of the fifties: one depicts a rolling pin, a flour sifter, a vase of daisies, and a cheerful, curly-headed mom wearing a red bead necklace; another shows a skillet, a milk bottle, a syrup pitcher, three eggs, and a grinning dad in an apron.

Oh, who are these people? My father never touched a spatula in his life. My mother suffered from "bad nerves," also "nervous stomach." She lived mostly on milk toast herself, yet she never failed to produce a nutritious supper for my father and me, including all the food groups, for she had long been a home economics teacher. Our perfect supper was ready every night at six thirty, the time a family ought to eat, in Mama's opinion, though my workaholic daddy never got home from the dimestore until eight or nine at the earliest, despite his best intentions. Somewhere in that two-hour stretch, I would have been allowed to eat alone, reading a book—my favorite thing in the world. My mother would have had her milk toast. And when my father finally had his solitary supper, warmed to an unrecognizable crisp in the oven, he never failed to pronounce it "absolutely delicious—the best thing I've ever put in my mouth!" My mother never failed to believe him, to give him her beautiful, tremulous smile, wearing the Fire and Ice lipstick she'd hurriedly applied when she heard his car in the driveway. Well, they loved each other—two sweet, fragile people who carefully bore this great love like a large glass object, incredibly delicate, along life's path.

My mother's father had died when she was only three, leaving a pile of debt and six children for my grandmother to raise alone on Chincoteague Island. Grandma Annie Marshall turned their big old Victorian home into a boardinghouse, and it was here in the boardinghouse kitchen that my mother had learned to cook. Her recipe box holds sixteen different recipes for oysters, including Oyster Stew, Oyster Fritters, Oyster Pie, Scalloped Oysters, and the biblical-sounding Balaam's Oysters. Clams are prepared "every whichaway," as she would have put it. There's also Planked Shad, Cooter Pie, and Pine Bark Stew. Mr. Hop Biddle's Hush Puppies bear the notation, "tossed to the hounds around the campfire to keep them quiet." Mama notes that the favorite breakfast at the boardinghouse was fried fish, corn-meal cakes, and "plenty of hot coffee." These cornmeal cakes remained her specialty from the time she was a little girl, barely able to reach the stove, until her death eighty-four years later in the mountains so far from her island home. I imagine her as a child, biting her bottom lip in concentration and wiping perspiration off her pretty little face as she flips those cornmeal cakes on the hot griddle. Later, I see her walking miles across the ice in winter, back to college on the mainland.

Her lofty aspirations were reflected in her recipes: Lady Balti-more Cake came from Cousin Nellie, who had "married well"; the hopeful Plantation Plum Pudding and Soiree Punch had both been contributed by my Aunt Gay-Gay in Birmingham, Alabama, the very epitome of something Mama had desperately wanted to attain. She wanted me to attain it, too, sending me down to Alabama every summer for Lady Lessons. The Aspara-gus Souffle recipe came from my elegant Aunt Millie, who had married a Northern steel executive who actually cooked dinner for us himself, wearing an apron. He produced a roast beef that was bright red in the middle; at first I was embarrassed for him, but then it turned out he'd meant to do it that way all along; he thought red meat was good, apparently, and enjoyed wearing the apron.

Here are Mama's bridge club recipes, filed all together. My first idea of an elegant meal came from this bridge club, whose members met every Thursday at noon for lunch and bridge, rotating houses, for years and years until its members began to die or move to Florida. I can see Mama now, greeting her friends at the door in her favorite black-and-white polka-dot dress. I sat on the top stair to watch them arrive. I loved the cut flowers, the silver, and the pink cloths on the tables, though it was clear to me even then that the way these ladies were was a way I'd never be.

The food my mama gave the bridge club was wonderful. They feasted upon molded pink salad that melted on the tongue (back then I thought all salads were Jell-O salads); something called Chicken Crunch (cut-up chicken, mushroom soup, celery, water chestnuts, Chinese noodles); and Lime Angel Cloud. All the bridge lunch recipes required mushroom soup, Jell-O, Dream Whip, or pecans.

But the recipes Mama actually used most—these soft, weathered index cards covered with thumbprints and spatters—reflect her deep involvement with her husband's family and their Appalachian community: Venison Stew, Gaynor Owens' Soup Beans, Ava McClanahan's Apple Stack Cake, my grandmother's

Methodist Church Supper Salad, and my favorite, Fid's Funeral Meat Loaf. A ham was also good in case of death, glazed with brown sugar and Coca-Cola. Mama's recipe for Salvation Cake had a Bible verse listed beside each ingredient (the almonds came from Genesis 43:11), and the only instruction given for baking was the cryptic Proverbs 23:14. Fat content was never a consideration. Biscuits called for lard, and Chocolate Velvet Cake required one cup of mayonnaise. A hearty beef and cheese casserole was named Husband's Delight.

I, too, have written out my life in recipes. As a young bride, I had eleven dessert recipes featuring Cool Whip as the main ingredient. Then came the hibachi and fondue period, then the quiche and crepes phase, then pasta, and now it's these salsa years. Just this past Christmas, I made cranberry salsa for everybody. My mother would not have touched salsa—let alone sushi!—with a ten-foot pole. One time when we all went out for bagels in Chapel Hill, she said, "This may taste good to someone who has never eaten a biscuit." Another thing she used to say is, "No matter what is wrong with you, a sausage biscuit will make you feel a whole lot better." I agree, though I have somehow ended up with a wonderful husband who eats rare meat, wears an apron himself upon occasion, and makes a terrific risotto. We share the cooking. I seldom have time to bake these days, but sometimes I still make Mama's Famous Loaf Bread upon occasion, simply because the smell of it baking takes me straight back to that warm kitchen where somebody

was always visiting. I can still hear my mother's voice, punctu-
ated by her infectious laugh, her conspiratorial "Now promise
me you won't tell a soul . . ."

On impulse I reach for Mama's recipe box and take out one
of the most wrinkled and smudged, Pimento Cheese, everybody's favorite, thinking as always that I really ought to get
these recipes into the computer, or at least copy them before
they disintegrate completely. On this card, Mama underlined
Durkee's Dressing, followed by a parenthesis: "(The secret ingredient!)" Though I would never consider leaving Durkee's
Dressing out, I don't really believe it is the secret ingredient.
The secret ingredient is love.

Kindly Nervous

"KINDLY NERVOUS" WAS MY FATHER'S euphemistic term for the immense anguish he suffered periodically from bipolar illness, or "manic depression," as it was then called. Unfortunately for him, the manic phase was no fun—no wild sprees, no elation—instead, he just worked harder than ever at the dimestore, where he did everything, anyway. When Daddy's mania increased to the point where he could no longer sleep, sometimes I accompanied him down to the store, sleeping on a pallet under his desk while he worked all night long, then going out with him into the chilly dawn to a greasy spoon for breakfast. How I loved those breakfasts! I got to have my scrambled eggs and my own big white china cup of sweet, milky coffee alongside early-morning truckers and the miners who'd just worked the graveyard shift, their eyes rimmed with coal dust like raccoons.

But these weeks of intense activity led to scarier behavior as he became increasingly jumpy and erratic. I remember one time when Daddy had taken me to the golf course in nearby Tazewell. I tossed him a putter when he wasn't expecting it, then was terrified when he screamed and fell down flat, writhing in tears on the putting green. Before long would come the inevitable downward spiral. He'd talk less and less, stay in bed more and more, finally be unable to go to the dimestore at all.

Then my Uncle Curt or my cousin Jack or another family member would come and drive him away to the hospital— sometimes the state mental hospital over in Marion, Virginia, sometimes an out-of-state facility. My father was lucky because he was in business with several men in his family who were willing to oversee the dimestore and his other responsibilities whenever he got "kindly nervous" and had to "go off" someplace to get treatment, since there was no mental health care—none at all—available in Buchanan County.

After I moved to North Carolina, we brought him down to Duke Hospital in Durham, very near us in Chapel Hill. I remember visiting him there once, in his third-floor room of the mental hospital wing, which overlooked the famous Duke Gardens, then in full bloom. He was not looking out at the gardens, though. Instead, I found him staring at a sheet of paper with something drawn on it.

"What's that?" I asked.

He replied that his doctor had left paper and pencil for him to draw a picture of a man doing something he enjoyed.

I looked at the stick figure. The man's hands hung straight down from his tiny hunched shoulders; his legs were straight parallel lines, up and down; his round head had no face, no features at all. None.

"So what's he doing?" I asked.

"Nothing," my father said.

In the fierce grip of severe depression, this popular, active, civic man—a great storyteller, a famous yellow-dog Democrat, a man who never knew a stranger—could not imagine doing anything . . . not one thing in the entire world that he might enjoy.

But the worst part was that he was always so horribly embarrassed about this illness, never understanding that it *was* an illness, but regarding it rather as a weakness, a failure of character, which made him feel even worse. "I can't believe I've gone and done this again," he'd say. "I'm just so ashamed of myself."

I will never forget what a breakthrough it was for him when I gave him William Styron's just-published book *Darkness Visible*, a memoir of Styron's own depression. My dad respected William Styron; he had read *The Confessions of Nat Turner*, he had heard Styron speak at a literary festival at my college. Daddy read *Darkness Visible* in one sitting.

"I can't believe it!" he said. "I can't believe he would tell these things!"

Styron had laid it on the line:

> Depression afflicts millions directly, and millions more who are relatives or friends of victims . . . as assertively democratic as a Norman Rockwell poster, it strikes indiscriminately at all ages, races, creeds, and classes . . . The pain of severe depression is quite unimaginable to those who have not suffered it, and it kills in many instances because its anguish can no longer be borne. The prevention of many suicides will continue to be hindered until there is a general awareness of the nature of this pain.

My mother, too, was hospitalized for depression and anxiety several times, mainly at Sheppard Pratt in Baltimore, but also at the University of Virginia Hospital in Charlottesville. She often attributed those bouts to "living with your father"—and undoubtedly there was some truth to this—but the fact is that she came from a "kindly nervous" family herself.

Her father and a brother both committed suicide; another brother, my Uncle Tick, was a schizophrenic who lived at home with my grandmother, then in the VA Hospital. An older cousin, Katherine, had died at the state mental institution in Staunton, Virginia, where she had been hospitalized because she was "over-sexed." (I never even knew this cousin had existed until many, many years later.) But I knew that Mama's beloved niece Andre was also in and out of the hospital in Washington frequently, suffering from schizophrenia. She died alone, too young, in her own apartment.

No wonder Mama and her sisters frequently took to their beds—just lying down wherever they lived, it seemed to me—whenever life got to be too much for them. Would I just lie down, too, I worried, when the time came? I was a whirlwind of energy, to counter this possibility.

When Mama got sick, she was physically sick, too—with stomach problems, insomnia, migraine headaches, and other undiagnosed pain. She ate very little and got very thin, subsisting on things she thought she could tolerate, such as rice, oatmeal, milk toast, and cream of wheat, which were all supposed to be easy on the stomach. In my memory, my mother's food was all white. She had a special daybed downstairs next to the kitchen, where she'd stay more and more. Ava McClanahan came every day to take care of Mama and the house. Daddy did all the shopping. This could go on for a long time. Sometimes Mama and I would be taken up to stay with my Aunt Millie and Uncle Bob in Maryland for a while. Other times, she went into the hospital.

This is my story, then, but it is not a sob story. Whenever either of my parents was gone, everybody—our relatives, neighbors, and friends—pitched in to help take care of me, bringing food over, driving me to Girl Scouts or school clubs or whatever else came up. People loved my parents, and in a mountain family and a small, isolated town like ours, that's just how people were. In times of trouble, they helped each other out. Also, I had my intense reading, and my writing, and usually a dog.

All their lives, my parents were kind, well-meaning people—heartbreakingly sweet. They did not understand their problems or what caused them. It is possible that they did not even understand their problems as illnesses, but they did not blame each other for them. Nor did they involve me in any way, other than trying to make sure that I would "get out" of whatever it was that they were "in"—Grundy, it often seemed to me, and I fought against this. I loved Grundy. But they were adamant, sending me away to summer camps and then to preparatory school, where they felt I would have "more advantages." Or maybe I was just too much for them, too lively, this child who came along so late in their lives.

Only once, the year I was thirteen, did my parents' hospitalizations coincide, when my father was at Silver Hill in Connecticut while my mother was at the University of Virginia Hospital in Charlottesville, and so I was sent to live with my Aunt Millie in Maryland. She enrolled me in a nearby "progressive, experimental" private school named Glenelg Country Day, where a friend of hers taught English. With thirty or forty students at most, Glenelg was situated in a grand old house—a mansion,

I thought at the time—surrounded by rolling fields. We called our teachers by their first names; meditated each morning; memorized a lot of poetry; and played a game I had never even seen before, called field hockey, with weird sticks. Everybody said I talked funny, but I thought they talked funny, too. I made some new friends and got to ride their horses, which I loved.

While I was there, I received an invitation from my mother's psychiatrist, a Dr. Stevenson, who proposed to take me out to lunch the next time I took the train down to visit my mother. In retrospect, this luncheon appears to me highly unusual, and I am surprised that my over-anxious Aunt Millie even allowed it. She customarily arranged for me to spend the night in Charlottesville with an old family friend whenever I went to visit Mama in the hospital, though neither the family friend nor my Aunt Millie had been invited to lunch. But Dr. Ian Stevenson was a well-known and respected physician, the new head of the Department of Psychiatry at the University of Virginia. He specialized in cases of psychosomatic illness—which must have included my mother.

Later, Dr. Stevenson would become famous for his interest in parapsychology, especially reincarnation. He thought that the concept of reincarnation might supplement what we know about heredity and environment in helping to understand aspects of behavior and development. He was especially interested in *Children Who Remember Previous Lives*, the title of a book he would publish in 1987. But if Dr. Stevenson had any curiosity about my own past lives, he kept mum about it. Our luncheon remains one of the most memorable occasions of my youth.

HE MET ME AT THE train station. He was a tall, angular man holding a pink rose, which he presented to me as he bowed. He was all dressed up in a suit and a vest and a tie. I was all dressed up, too, in my pleated plaid skirt and navy blue jacket and Add-A-Pearl necklace. Dr. Stevenson put me and my little bag into his big, shiny car and took me to a fancy restaurant up on a hill, with linen tablecloths. He told me to order anything I wanted from the largest menu I had ever seen. I chose lemonade and a club sandwich, which arrived in four fat triangles with a little flag stuck into each one, plus curly potato chips and pickles. I ate every bite.

Dr. Stevenson said that he had heard a lot about me from my mother, and he had wanted to meet me because he thought that I must be an interesting little girl. He asked me a lot of questions about my new school, and what books I liked to read, listening very carefully to my answers. I had just read *Jane Eyre* twice, cover to cover. Dr. Stevenson nodded as if this were the very thing to do. I loved poetry, I told him. Then I recited the poem we had just learned, "'Breathes there the man, with soul so dead, Who never to himself hath said, This is my own, my native land?'" I took a deep breath and followed that one up with "Annabel Lee" in its entirety. Nobody could have stopped me. "It sounds like a wonderful school," Dr. Stevenson said, smiling.

Then Dr. Stevenson leaned forward intently and said, "Lee, since your parents are both ill, I wonder if you have ever worried about getting sick as well."

"You mean, if I am going to go crazy, too," I blurted out.

"Yes," he said, "if you are going to go crazy, too."

I stared across the table at him. How did he *know*? because that was exactly what I thought about, of course, all the time.

"Yes!" I said.

"Well, I am a very good doctor," he said, "and you seem to me to be a very nice, normal little girl, and I am here to tell you that you can stop worrying about this right now. So you can just relax, and read a lot more books, and grow up. You will be fine."

I sank back in my chair.

"Now," he said, "would you like some dessert?"

"Yes," I said.

The waitress brought the giant menus back.

I ordered Baked Alaska, which I had never heard of, and was astonished when it arrived in flames. The waitress held it out at arms' length, then set it down right in front of me. It looked like a big fiery cake. "Oh no!" I cried, scooting my chair back. Everybody in the restaurant was pointing and laughing at me. Even Dr. Stevenson was laughing.

"You're supposed to blow it out," the waitress said.

I tried, but the more I blew, the higher the flames went, and the more they jumped around. I felt like I was at some weird birthday party where everything had gone horribly wrong. "I can't," I said finally. Dr. Stevenson stood up, his expression changing to concern. Out of the corner of my eye, I could see waitresses and kitchen staff converging upon our table. I could feel the heat on my face. I blew and blew, but the Baked Alaska would not go out.

Lady Lessons

WHEN I WAS A LITTLE GIRL, my mother drove me all the
way across the entire state of Virginia to visit my Grandmother
Marshall and my Aunt Millie and Millie's best friend, Bobbie,
in Baltimore. This annual trip was part of my mother's grand
plan; she was raising me to be a lady. The drive took two days
with my mother at the wheel. We broke our trip by staying
with Mama's friend Frances at Port Republic in the Valley of
Virginia. My mother always said "the Valley of Virginia" in a
certain way, with a certain tilt of the head. Frances's family lived
in a huge house, a plantation really, with a white-columned
portico and a long view out over the golden, rolling land.

These summer journeys symbolized the difference between
my parents. Mama was a real lady from the Eastern Shore of
Virginia, where her father had been in the oyster business. He

was a high roller and harness racer. A picture of him hung in our sitting room: a handsome man with a big mustache, dressed to the nines, standing tall and straddle-legged atop what appears to be a small mountain of oyster shells. He carries a silver-headed cane; he wears a dark broad-brimmed hat; the drooping gold chain of his watch hangs down from his pocket. A man of consequence, of style. The family lived in a substantial square white house with sidewalk and street in front, green lawn sloping down to the Chesapeake Bay behind. In the backyard stood the summer kitchen, the smokehouse, the icehouse, the cistern for catching rainwater, the little train my grandfather had constructed mostly for his children and his own amusement, which carried loads of mainland goods and groceries from dock to house. (In those days before the Bay Bridge was built, the only way to the mainland was by boat. In winter, Mama said, she had to "walk the ice" to get back to Madison Teachers College after her Christmas vacation.)

My mother was named Virginia Elizabeth Marshall, called "Gig," and she was, I have to say, an absolutely adorable young woman. Early photographs show a mop of unruly dark curls, huge blue eyes, a carefree smile, and deep, mischievous dimples. Her flapper-style looks exactly fit the prevailing beauty ideal of the day. No wonder my father fell madly in love with her at first sight and brought her home to Grundy, to those peaks and hollers where she would feel a little bit out of place forever, even though she adored him. And he adored her. In fact, as a child I was horribly embarrassed by the Technicolor-movie-style quality of my parents' passionate marriage.

I remember one bright summer Sunday when my cousins gave me a ride back from Sunday school—for some reason, my parents had stayed at home. I ran down our flagstone walk, burst into the house, and yelled, "Hello! I'm back!" but the sunlit living room seemed strangely empty. I went into the kitchen, following my nose. I smelled bacon and coffee. Sure enough, their breakfast plates were still on the table. This was not at all like Mama, the best housekeeper in the world. Maybe they had been kidnapped by aliens, I thought, which happened frequently in the pages of the *National Enquirer*, which Mama and I loved.

"Mama?" I called. "Daddy?"

Nothing.

Yet a thin blue haze of their cigarette smoke still hung in the air. "Mama?" I looked out on the back porch and into the backyard where her beloved roses bloomed. Nobody. "Daddy!" I yelled.

"Why, honey, what's the matter?" Suddenly they were there. Mama bent down to kiss me, with Daddy right behind her. Yet something was wrong with them, I could tell. Mama's pansy-sprigged blouse was buttoned up wrong, her red lipstick slapped on a little askew, while Daddy just stood there in the door-way as if in a trance, smiling at Mama, not at me—not at me, who had been so worried, so scared! The next day, at school, I

told everybody I was an orphan. ("No you're not," my patient
teacher said.)

A YEAR OR SO LATER, when I was sick, I woke up suddenly
in the middle of the night with my throat on fire. I headed for
their bedroom, knowing that Mama would get up and give
me an aspirin and put Mentholatum on my chest and a cold
washcloth on my forehead, and maybe even dose me up with
some of her surefire cough medicine—a spoonful of honey and
bourbon. But their bedroom door stood ajar, the lamp burning
on the bedside table. The chenille bedspread lay undisturbed
on their carefully made bed—clearly, it had not been slept in.
I checked the clock: 1:15. I padded down the hall and paused at
the narrow back staircase where suddenly I heard music. I crept
downstairs, with Nancy Drew–like stealth, until I could see
them—dancing barefoot in the kitchen! How gross, I thought;
they were old. I plopped down on the step in disgust.

My parents were jitterbugging wildly to the Louisiana rhythm
of Hank Williams singing, "Jambalaya and a crawfish pie and
filé gumbo . . . Son of a gun, we'll have big fun on the bayou!"
Daddy would pull her to him, then swing her around. Her red
skirt flew out on the turns. They were wonderful dancers. Then
the record changed to that sad whippoorwill song and Daddy
pulled her close and they were dancing cheek to cheek, dipping
and gliding around the kitchen floor. Now he held her in a tight

embrace. "The moon just went behind the clouds . . . I'm so lonesome I could cry," Hank Williams's mournful voice floated up the stairs. I started crying myself. I snuck back to bed where I lay in quivering pain and silence for a long time. Maybe I'm having a nervous breakdown, I thought, like Jane Eyre when they put her in the Red Room.

Mama was a very popular teacher at the high school; even boys signed up for her home economics classes. Years later, at her funeral, one man stood up and said that he had "gone to school to Miss Gig," and announced that she was "real nice, for a foreigner"—this despite the fact that she had been married to my father and had lived in Grundy for over fifty years.

I WAS NOT A FOREIGNER. I was my daddy's girl through and through, a mountain girl, a born tomboy who loved Grundy and everything about it, especially in the summertime when I was part of a wild gang of neighborhood children who roamed from house to house, ran the mountains as we pleased, and generally enjoyed a degree of freedom that it is almost impossible now to imagine. Summer spread out all around us like another country, ours to plunder and explore. Aside from chores and one week of compulsory Bible School (red Kool-Aid, Lorna Doone cookies, lanyards) we were on our own. We had no day camps, no lessons, no car pools. We played roll-to-bat, kick-ball, Red Rover, dodge ball, Pretty Girl Station, tag, statues, hidey-go-seek. I was utterly fearless in those days; I could run like the wind, and hit like a boy.

Sometimes I wrote plays, which we'd all put on in the breezeway at Martha's house, using a quilt on a clothesline as the curtain. Some of the more fundamentalist parents got very upset, I remember, at one particular production named *The Drunken Saloon* that ended with all of us, cowboys and cowgirls alike, pretending to be passed out cold on the concrete floor.

Inspired by Nancy Drew, my cousins and I concocted an elaborate ongoing plot concerning a mystery train that ran around the tops of the mountains and an evil group of invisible beings who were inhabiting the bodies of townspeople we didn't like. We spied on these people and kept official notebooks filled with our clues and "findings," written in code.

One time my cousin Randy and I pushed an old oil drum off its rusty perch at an abandoned tipple and watched with great satisfaction as it crashed down the mountainside, gathering speed, then crossed the road and slammed into a filling station, where luckily nobody was hurt.

Sometimes my daddy took me up on Compton Mountain to ride the mine ponies, blind from their years underground. Often I'd go to town with him and work in the dimestore. But mostly summer consisted of roaming the mountains with the other kids—"like little wild animals," Mama said in disgust—building forts, waging wars, and playing make-believe games of every description. Sometimes we'd flatten out cardboard boxes and take them up to the tree line where we'd sit on them, holding the front up to form a kind of sled, and slide down the long sage-grass hillside to the road, then trudge back up again. After a few rides, the flattened grass would be really slick. We would do this all afternoon.

Despite my inclinations, my mother kept at it, trying her best to raise me to be a lady. She sent me to visit my lovely Aunt Gay-Gay in Birmingham, Alabama, every summer for two weeks of honest-to-God Lady Lessons. Here I'd learn how to wear white gloves, sit up straight, and walk in little Cuban heels. I'd learn proper table manners, which would then be tested by fancy lunches at "The Club" on top of Shades Mountain. I'd learn the rules: "A lady does not point. A lady eats before the party. A lady never lets a silence fall. A lady always wears clean underwear in case she is in a wreck. A lady does not sit *like that*!"

I didn't want to be a lady, of course; I wanted to be a boy.

EVEN THOUGH OUR VISITS TO Baltimore were a part of Mama's grand design, I enjoyed them. I loved Baltimore itself, with its clanging streetcars, funny-looking people, lamplights, pigeons, and ice cream cones. I loved to sit out on the marble stoop after dinner and watch the teeming parade of street life; I always had a nickel in my pocket just in case the organ-grinder came by with his monkey. This monkey wore a little green coat with brass buttons. I loved my sweet, refined grandmother in her dim, high-ceilinged row house with lace at the windows and doilies on the tables. She always referred to my late grandfather with great respect, often making such statements as "Mr. Marshall raised trotters, you know" or "Mr. Marshall loved oysters in any form." This deference enchanted me.

Much, much later, I was astonished to learn that Mr. Marshall had, in fact, hanged himself when my mother was five years old and Millie was only three, leaving my grandmother alone with a half a dozen young children to raise. She'd turned their house into a boardinghouse; later, she'd sold it and followed Millie to Baltimore, where everybody's favorite cousin, Nellie, had made a brilliant marriage and lived in style, with—of all things—a butler! Family legend tells that I'd been instructed again and again how to behave in the presence of this butler before I was first presented to him; then I'd disgraced everyone by rolling on the floor.

In my own memory, my elegant Aunt Millie was always re-ferred to as an "executive secretary," a phrase that fascinated me, as there was no such thing in Grundy. I loved my Aunt Mille, but I absolutely worshipped her friend Bobbie, the most glamorous woman I'd ever seen.

In hushed tones, my mother informed me that Bobbie was

a divorcee; back home, there was no such thing as that, either. Bobbie was said to be a crackerjack stenographer. She was a tall woman with stylishly cut suits featuring big shoulders and tiny waists. She wore stiletto heels, stockings with black seams up the back, and red lipstick. She had the long, lovely legs of a fashion model, and—best of all—lacquered hair, which she wore up, in a jaunty French twist. It looked like patent leather.

Despite these attributes, Bobbie was reputed to be "unlucky in love," an expression that never failed to send a great dark thrill shooting through me. During our visits, Mama and Millie and Bobbie always sat up late and giggled and blew smoke rings and drank Black Russians, and talked about men. I'd fall asleep to the muffled sound of their squeals and laughter.

My grandmother died when I was about ten. This time, our long trip was a sad one. My father drove, my mother cried. They both smoked cigarettes all the way, filling our fishtailed car with a blue haze indistinguishable from the constant rain outside. I was asleep when we got there, waking at noon to hear myself deemed "too young to go to the funeral." Bobbie would stay with me.

I will never forget that long afternoon, which I spent sitting on the horsehair sofa looking out at the rain and the row houses opposite us while Bobbie drank red wine and railed against the latest "jerk" who had betrayed her. She wore black silk pants and a lime green sleeveless angora sweater.

"Listen," she said, stabbing out a cigarette. "Never, ever, trust a man who says, 'Trust me.'"

Then her mood changed abruptly. "Well," she said, "we've got all afternoon. You might as well learn to dance." She got up and crossed the room to the record player.

"Come here," she said, and I did. "Now stand like this. Put your hand on my waist. Good. Now put your other hand on my shoulder, like this." I did. "Okay," she said. "Follow me."

We glided off into the dramatic opening of "Begin the Beguine." It was easy, easy. I imitated Bobbie's proud carriage, the reckless set of her crimson mouth, and my legs moved of their own accord across the flowered, threadbare carpet. Round and round we went, now to "Deep Purple": "when the deep purple falls over sleepy garden walls, and the stars begin to twinkle in the sky . . ."

I REMEMBERED MY PARENTS, DANCING in our kitchen. I could imagine my grandmother dancing with the doomed and dashing Mr. Marshall. And suddenly, for the first time, I could imagine myself, dancing with a man whose face I could not yet see. For despite Bobbie's warning, I would grow up to love several men, some of them trustworthy and some of them not—though perhaps I would never love anybody else in quite the same way I loved Bobbie herself that afternoon of my grandmother's funeral, as we swept back and forth across the darkening apartment to those old sweet strains . . . "Through the mist of a memory, you wander back to me, breathing my name with a sigh . . ." while her angora sweater brushed my cheek like angels' wings.

Marble Cake and Moonshine

ALTHOUGH I DON'T USUALLY write autobiographical fiction, the main character in one of my short stories sounds suspiciously like the girl I used to be: "More than anything else in the world, I wanted to be a writer. I didn't want to learn to write, of course. I just wanted to be a writer, and I often pictured myself poised at the foggy edge of a cliff someplace in the south of France, wearing a cape, drawing furiously on a long cigarette, hollow-cheeked and haunted. I had been romantically dedicated to the grand idea of 'being a writer' ever since I could remember."

I had started telling stories as soon as I could talk—true stories, and made-up stories, too. My father was fond of saying that I would climb a tree to tell a lie rather than stand on the ground to tell the truth. In fact, a lie was often called a "story" in southwest Virginia, and well do I remember being shaken until my teeth rattled with the stern admonition, "Don't you tell me no story, now!"

But I couldn't help it. I got hooked on stories early, and as soon as I could write, I started writing them down, first on my mother's Crane stationery when I was about nine, later in little books with covers I carefully made for them, pasting on pictures I'd cut out of magazines or catalogs, or illustrating them myself. I wrote my way through school, fueled by my voracious reading. I'd read anything: mysteries, romances, true crime, science fiction, all the books that came to our house from the Book of the Month Club. Finally at St. Catherine's School in Richmond, during my last two years of high school, I was gently but firmly guided into the classics, though my own fiction remained relentlessly sensational.

At Hollins College, I wrote about stewardesses living in Hawaii (where I had never been), about orphans, evil twins, fashion models, and alternative universes, receiving Bs and Cs and cryptic little comments from my professors Lex Allen and Richard Dillard that said, basically, "Write what you know." I thought this was terrible advice. I didn't know what they meant. I didn't know what I knew. All I knew was that I was not going to write anything about Grundy, Virginia, ever, that was for sure. My last glimpse of home had been my mother and two of her friends sitting on the porch drinking iced tea and talking (endlessly) about whether one of them ought to have a hysterectomy or not. Well! I was outta there!

But I was still drunk on words and books, just as I had been as a child, when I used to read under the covers with a flashlight all night long. My favorite professor at Hollins was Louis D. Rubin, Jr., who introduced us to Southern literature; I hadn't even known it existed when we started out. I had already gotten drunk on Faulkner a couple of times, then had to go to the infirmary for a whole day when we read William Styron's *Lie Down in Darkness*—I got too "wrought up," as my mother used to say. The nurse gave me a tranquilizer, and made me lie down.

Even so, I considered cutting class on the day that this woman with a funny name, from Mississippi, was coming to visit us. She was on campus, I believe, to receive the Hollins Medal, an honor undoubtedly engineered by Mr. Rubin, one of her earliest and greatest champions. But I had never heard of her, and it was so pretty outside, a great day to cut class and go up to Carvins Cove and drink some beer or just stomp moodily around campus smoking cigarettes and acting like a writer. This was my plan until I ran into Mr. Rubin in the campus post office, and then I had to go to class.

There were a lot more people in that old high-ceilinged classroom than we had ever had before, and some of them were male, a rarity at Hollins in those days. The seats in the back of the room were filling up fast with faculty from our own college and from other area colleges, too, (beards, leather patches on the elbows of their ratty sports jackets: not your dad) as well as graduate students from UVA and W&L. The graduate students needed haircuts, and looked intense. In fact they looked exactly like the fabled sixties, reputed to be happening somewhere outside our fairytale Blue Ridge campus at that very time.

A ripple of anticipation ran through the crowd. Mr. Rubin was ushering Eudora Welty into the room.

I was deeply disappointed. Why, she certainly didn't look like a writer! She didn't have a cape, or boots, or anything. What she wore was one of those nice-lady linen dresses that buttoned up the front, just like all the other nice ladies I had known in my life, just like my mother and all her friends. In fact, she looked a little bit like Miss Nellie Hart, my eighth-grade English teacher. (My favorite English teacher ever, but still . . .) I lost interest immediately.

I can't remember what Mr. Rubin said when he introduced her; I was probably too busy stealing glances at the back of the room while appearing not to.

Then Eudora Welty began to read "A Worn Path" out loud in her fast light voice that seemed to sing along with the words of the story. And I was suddenly right there—in Mississippi with Phoenix Jackson as she sets out to get the medicine for her grandson, encountering the thorny bush, the scarecrow, and the black dog, the young hunter and the lady along the way. I could see that "pearly cloud of mistletoe" near the beginning and then Phoenix's little grandson near the end: "He got a sweet look. He going to last. He wear a little patch quilt and peep out holding his mouth open like a little bird." I sat stunned when it was over.

Miss Welty had seemed perfectly composed as she was reading; her face was luminous, lit from within. Now, having finished, she looked nearly shy, though her huge blue eyes were shining. "Well," she said, looking all around, "any questions?" Hands waved everywhere.

She chose the young man who seemed the most impassioned. Knowing what I know now, I'll bet anything his dissertation was riding on his question. He leapt to his feet to ask it.

"I wonder," he said, his dark curly hair going everywhere, "if you could comment upon your choice of marble cake as a symbol of the fusion between dream and reality, between the temporal and the eternal, the male and the female, the union of yin and yang . . ." He made yin-yang motions with his hands.

Miss Welty smiled sweetly at him. "Well," she said slowly, considering, "it's a lovely cake, and it's a recipe that has been in my family for years."

Marble cake! My own mother made the best marble cake in town.

It would be years before I would understand that exchange, and what really took place in our classroom that day. Later, in the final section of *One Writer's Beginnings*, Miss Welty would put it best when she wrote that "the outside world is the vital component of my inner life. My work, in the terms in which I can see it, is as dearly matched to the world as its secret sharer.

My imagination takes its strength and guides its direction from what I see and hear and learn and feel and remember of my living world."

Immediately after Miss Welty's visit, I read everything she had ever written. And it was like that proverbial lightbulb clicked on in my head—suddenly, I knew what I knew! With the awful arrogance of the nineteen-year-old, I decided that Eudora Welty hadn't been anywhere much either, and yet she wrote the best stories I had ever read. Plain stories about country people and small towns—my own "living world." I sat down and wrote a little story myself, about three women sitting on a porch drinking iced tea and talking endlessly about whether one of them does or does not need a hysterectomy. I got an *A* on it.

BASED ON EUDORA WELTY'S influence upon my own beginnings, I have always felt that one of the most important functions of any good writing teacher is to serve as a sort of matchmaker—"fixing up" a new writer with the fiction of a successful published author whose work comes out of a similar background, place, sensibility, or life experience. A certain resonance, or recognition, occurs. This can be an important step in finding a voice. Especially when we are just starting out, we encounter other writers who are like lighthouses for us.

For instance, when I introduced young Kentucky writer Silas House to the work of Larry Brown. Silas recalls, "*Father and Son* had a profound impact on me. The way his characters were so intertwined with place—they couldn't be separated. I recall shortly after reading the book that a major reviewer said Brown wrote 'about the characters with whom you'd never want to have supper.' I thought: 'Those are the folks I've been eating with my whole life!' And so Larry's work really gave me permission to write about my people in all of their gritty glory, a grit formed by the rough land where we lived."

But even though my reading of Eudora Welty had led me to abandon my stewardesses, setting my feet on more familiar ground, telling simpler stories about small-town Southern life, I was never able, somehow, to set my first stories in those deep mountains I came from, or to write in my first language, the beautiful and precise Appalachian dialect I had grown up hearing as a child.

This did not happen until I encountered James Still—all by myself, actually, perusing the *S*s in the Hollins College library.

Here I found the beautiful and heartbreaking novel *River of Earth*, a kind of Appalachian *The Grapes of Wrath* chronicling the Baldridge family's desperate struggle to survive when the mines close and the crops fail, familiar occurrences in Appalachian life. Theirs is a constant odyssey, always looking for something better someplace else—a better job, a better place to live, a promised land. As the mother says, "Forever moving, yon and back, setting down nowhere for good and all, searching for God knows what. Where are we expecting to draw up to?"

At the end of the novel, I was astonished to read that the family was heading for—of all places!—*Grundy*.

"I was born to dig coal," Father said. "Somewhere they's a mine working. I been hearing of a new mine farther than the head of Kentucky River, on yon side Pound Gap. Grundy, its name is . . ."

I read this passage over and over. I simply could not believe that Grundy was in a novel! In print! Published! Then I finished reading *River of Earth* and burst into tears. Never had I been so moved by a book. In fact it didn't seem like a book at all. That novel was as real to me as the chair I sat on, as the hollers I'd grown up among, as the voices of my kinfolk.

Suddenly, lots of the things of my own life occurred to me for the first time as stories: my great-granddaddy's "other family" in West Virginia; Hardware Breeding, who married his wife, Beulah, four times; how my Uncle Vern taught my daddy to drink good liquor in a Richmond hotel; how I got saved at the tent revival; John Hardin's hanging in the courthouse square; how Petey Chaney rode the flood; the time Mike Holland and I went to the serpent-handling church in Jolo; the murder Daddy saw when he was a boy, out riding his little pony—and never told . . .

I started to write these stories down. Many years later, I'm still at it. And it's a funny thing: Though I have spent most of my working life in universities, though I live in piedmont North Carolina now and eat pasta and drive a Subaru, the stories that present themselves to me as worth the telling are often those somehow connected to that place and those people. The mountains that used to imprison me have become my chosen stalking ground.

THIS IS THE PLACE WHERE James Still lived most of his life, in an old log house built in the 1800s between Wolfpen Creek and Dead Mare Branch near Wolfpen, accessible only by eight miles of dirt road and two miles of creek bed. Still was born into a farm family of five sisters and four brothers in Alabama in 1906; went to Lincoln Memorial University near Cumberland Gap, Tennessee, where he worked as a janitor in the library to earn his scholarship and discovered *The Atlantic* magazine, which he read cover to cover, every issue. Later he would publish ten stories and several poems in the very magazine that he had read so carefully. He earned another bachelor's degree in library science at the University of Illinois at Urbana–Champaign and a master's in English at Vanderbilt, but was still unable to get a job in the midst of the great Depression. After picking cotton and riding the rails, he came to Knott County, Kentucky, in 1932, where he finally found employment at the Hindman Settlement School, an association that would last for the rest of his long life. As the librarian, he carried books to people all over remote Knott County, working for room and board only. Eventually the school paid him $15 a month, and he began to sell his poems and stories to magazines nationwide. He also worked for the Federal Emergency Relief Administration, traveling the county on foot, talking to everybody, writing their stories down in his ever-present notebook.

After six years, as he liked to tell it, he "retired" and turned to reading and writing full-time. As one of his neighbors said, "He's quit a good job and come over in here and sot down." Another called him "the man in the bushes," and yet another suspected him of "devilish writing." But he was a gardener and a beekeeper as well, soon becoming almost like a family member of his dulcimer-making neighbors, the Amburgeys. Though not locally read, he was locally accepted. He talked to everybody, at every opportunity—at country stores, pie suppers, and the like. "You may talk smart, but you've got hillbilly wrote all over you," one man told him. His neighbors' writings and sayings appeared in *The Wolfpen Notebooks*, published in 1991.

When the nearby Hindman Settlement School started its now-famous Appalachian Writers' Workshop, I had the immense pleasure of getting to know Mr. Still and becoming his friend, from my first visit there in the seventies until his death in 2001, when we buried him up on the mountain above the school. We always called him "Mr. Still," all of us—even Mike Mullins, who ran the Settlement School and knew Mr. Still better and longer than anybody. The continuing Appalachian Writers Workshop gave me (and many others) an Appalachian community of the heart, just as Mr. Still gave us all the example of a real writer, not in it for money or fame but for the love of the language and the telling of the truth as he saw it. Deeply erudite, he once told me he had read an average of three hours a day, every day, for over seventy years. He was a world traveller who had visited twenty-six countries, yet he was as interested in the sayings and doing of his neighbors as he was in the Mayan culture of Central America, where he returned time after time. Though *River of Earth* (1940) remained his masterpiece, his short stories and poetry were widely and justly praised as well, appearing not only in *The Atlantic* but also in *The Yale Review, Saturday Review, The Saturday Evening Post, Esquire*, and many other publications, textbooks, and anthologies. He loved children and also wrote for them—*Sporty Creek, Jack and the Wonder Beans*—and in his later years I had the honor of helping him get together a collection of his Appalachian Mother Goose poems.

Mr. Still never married, but loved women, even at ninety. I will always treasure a note he wrote to me then in his firm, inimitable handwriting: "Dear Lee, When are you getting here? Let's ride around. Love, Jim." We liked to sip a little moonshine or bourbon in paper cups while driving his big old Lincoln over the mountain to Hazard for a restaurant steak. Just before his death, Mr. Still wrote, asking me to come and "pick up a little old leather suitcase I've got up here someplace"; the suitcase turned out to contain the handwritten, jumbled manuscript of

Chinaberry, a novel he had written years before, a mysterious story he had often repeated to all of us there on the porch after dinner, about being taken to Texas as a child to pick cotton. Now it has been beautifully edited by Silas House and published by the University of Kentucky Press.

What is it about Appalachia that so captures the mind, echoes in the ear, and lodges in the heart? An old woman once told me, "Well, there's just more *there* there." In the preface to his *The Wolfpen Notebooks*, Mr. Still wrote:

> Appalachia is that somewhat mythical region with no known borders. If such an area exists in terms of geography, such a domain as has shaped the lives and endeavors of men and women from pioneer days to the present and given them an independence and an outlook and a vision such as is often attributed to them, I trust to be understood for imagining the heart of it to be in the hills of eastern Kentucky where I have lived and feel at home and where I have exercised as much freedom and peace as the world allows.

This is an enviable life, to live in the terrain of one's heart. Most writers don't—can't—do this. Most of us are always searching, through our work and in our lives: for meaning, for love, for home.

Writing is about these things. And as writers, we cannot choose our truest material. But sometimes we are lucky enough to find it.

HERITAGE

I shall not leave these prisoning hills
Though they topple their barren heads to level earth
And the forests slide uprooted out of the sky.
Though the waters of Troublesome, of Trace Fork,
Of Sand Lick rise in a single body to glean the valleys,
To drown lush pennyroyal, to unravel rail fences;
Though the sun-ball breaks the ridges into dust
And burns its strength into the blistered rock
I cannot leave. I cannot go away.

Being of these hills, being one with the fox
Stealing into the shadows, one with the new-born foal,
The lumbering ox drawing green beech logs to mill,
One with the destined feet of man climbing and descending,
And one with death rising to bloom again, I cannot go.
Being of these hills I cannot pass beyond.

—James Still

Big River

Sometimes life is more like a river than a book.
—Cort Conley

IN MY NOVEL *The Last Girls*, the trip starts like this (imagine a winter afternoon on the historic campus of a women's college in Virginia; imagine a group of girls discussing *Hucklebery Finn* around a table in their American Literature seminar) . . .

Another day, Mr. Gaines read from the section where Huck and Jim are living on the river:

Sometimes we'd have that whole river to ourselves for the longest time. Yonder was the banks and the islands, across the water, and maybe a spark—which was a candle in a cabin window . . . and maybe you could hear a fiddle or a song coming over from one of them crafts. It's lovely to live on a raft.

His words had rung out singly, like bells, in the old classroom. Harriet could hear each one in her head. It was a cold pale day in February. Out the window, bare trees stood blackly amid the gray tatters of snow.

Then Baby had said, "I'd love to do that. Go down the Mississippi River on a raft, I mean." It was a typical response from Baby, who personalized everything, who was famous for saying, "Well, I'd never do that!" at the end of *The Awakening* when Edna Pontellier walks into the ocean. Baby was not capable of abstract thought. She had too much imagination. Everything was real for her, close up and personal.

"We could do it, you know," Suzanne St. John spoke up. "My uncle owns a plantation right on the river, my mother was raised there. She'd know who to talk to. I'll bet we could do it if we wanted to." Next to Courtney, Suzanne St. John was the most organized girl in school, an angular, forthright girl with a businesslike grownup hairdo who ran a mail-order stationery business out of her dorm room.

"Girls, girls," Mr. Gaines had said disapprovingly. He wanted to get back to the book, he wanted to be the star. But the girls were all looking at each other. Baby's eyes were shining. *"Yes!"* she wrote on a piece of paper, handing it to Harriet, who passed it along to Suzanne. Yes. This was Baby's response to everything.

That's an excerpt from the novel. But this is the truth.

The summer after my junior year at Hollins, I actually did go down the Mississippi River on a raft with fifteen other girls, inspired by reading *Huckleberry Finn* in Louis Rubin's American literature class. This trip was organized by the indomitable senior Patricia Neild from Shreveport, but might not have happened without the help of a sophomore named Vicki Derby, whose old New Orleans family had invaluable ties up and down the river. Underlying the entire project was the subliminal message that Hollins had been giving us all along: that we could do anything, if we worked hard enough for it. Girls could do anything. We browbeat all our families for cash, then raised more any way we could think of, including loans and endorsements for various products. We made actual commercials for Chicken of the Sea tuna, Rayovac batteries, and Wrangler jeans.

On June 9th, 1966, we launched the *Rosebud Hobson* at Paducah, Kentucky, and headed 950 miles down the Ohio and Mississippi Rivers to New Orleans. The *Rosebud Hobson* was a forty-by-sixteen-foot wooden platform built on fifty-two oil drums and powered by two forty-horsepower motors. It cost us eighteen hundred dollars to build. We had a superstructure of two-by-fours with a tarpaulin top that we could pull over it, mosquito netting that we could hang up, and a shower consisting of a bucket overhead with a long rope attached to it. The raft was named for an early Hollins College alumna from Paducah, a pianist whose European career had involved some mysterious "tragedy," according to her sister, Miss Lillian Hobson, who entertained us before the launch.

Our captain was a retired riverboat pilot named Gordon S.

Cooper. We painted rosebuds all over the raft and sang, "Good-bye, Paducah" to the tune of "Hello, Dolly" as we left. In fact, we sang relentlessly all the time, all the way down the Mississippi.

We sang in spite of all our mishaps and travails: the tail of a hurricane that hit us before we even got to Cairo, sending the temperature down below forty degrees and driving us onto the rocks; a diet consisting almost entirely of tuna and doughnuts; the captain's severe sunburn, requiring medical care; mosquito bites beyond belief and rainstorms that soaked everything we owned despite the useless tarp. If anything really bad happened to us, we figured we could call up our parents collect, and they would come and fix things. We expected to be taken care of. Nobody had ever suggested to us that we might ever have to make a living, or that somebody wouldn't marry us and then look after us for the rest of our lives. We all smoked cigarettes. We were all cute. We headed down that river with absolute confidence that we would get where we were going.

We worked and fished and played cards and talked and talked and talked. It was wonderful. In between stints as cook and keeper of the ship log, I was writing my own first novel. I had it all outlined, and every day I sat down crosslegged on deck and wrote five or six pages of it, on a yellow legal pad. I followed my outline absolutely. In creative writing class, I had learned how plot works: beginning, middle, and end; conflict, complication, and resolution.

Huck, our inspiration, was an American Odysseus off on an archetypal journey—the oldest plot of all. According to the archetype, the traveler learns something about himself (not herself) along the way. What was I learning? Not much. Only that if you are cute and sing a lot of songs, people will come out whenever you dock and bring you pound cake and ham and beer and keys to the city, and when you get to New Orleans you will be met by the band from Preservation Hall on a tugboat, and showered by red roses dropped from a helicopter, paid for by somebody's daddy.

In all my yellowed newspaper clippings, the press refers to us as "girls"; today, of course, they'd call us "women." We were the last girls. In 1966, a lot of things were changing for good, though we didn't know it yet. More possibilities and opportunities for women would bring greater expectations and responsibilities—along with a lack of both illusions and stability. Whatever happened to romance, for instance? or the sacred Fifties Family?

Over the years, many people asked when I was going to write about the raft trip—it seemed like such a natural. Why, we'd been famous at the time, appearing nationally on *Huntley-Brinkley*, covered by every TV station up and down the river and by every newspaper in the South. A three-column closeup photograph of me had appeared on the front page of the Memphis *Commercial Appeal*, wearing a bandana on my head, cut-off jeans, my Rosebud Hobson T-shirt and a big grin, smoking a cigarette. (When somebody sent this clipping to my mother, she went to bed immediately.)

In that picture, I was clearly having the time of my life. We all were. But this was the problem, this was why the raft trip was not a natural for fiction, even though the journey is, of course, the archetypal plot for a novel or a story. Somebody once said that there are only two plots in fiction. The first is, somebody takes a trip (*The Iliad, The Odyssey, Don Quixote, Huckleberry Finn, Heart of Darkness*). The second one is, a stranger comes to town (*Absalom, Absalom; The Great Gatsby; The Glass Menagerie*). If you think about it, this is absolutely true.

But a trip—or a plot, let us say—is merely a series of events, and even the most interesting events do not add up to a story. We have to know who these events are happening to, and the better we know this person, the more we will care about what happens to him, the more we will want to read his story. There is a big difference between a plot and a story. A story requires not only events, but character, theme, meaning—and above all, conflict. Conflict is the essential difference between fiction and all other types of prose narrative. For fiction is a structured imitation of life, not life itself. Fiction organizes and reforms the raw material of fact to emphasize and clarify what is most significant in life for its characters. What do they want? What do they love?—hope for?—fear? What is up for grabs in the world of this story? What do these events mean to these characters? Because frequently, their lives will be forever changed by the events of the story. In any case, the possibility of change must arise: that's conflict, and without conflict, fiction does not exist.

The story happens at the point where event and character converge—or, more frequently, collide. The story tells how events affect and change the character (s), and how the character(s) affect and change events. The events of the story must mean something to the characters—or at the very least, to the reader, who is sometimes able to discern a pattern in these events that the character himself cannot see or understand.

So . . . taking a trip, even the best trip in the world, with the best companions, is not enough. Fact is, we had a great time on the raft. Period. And that was not a story. But years passed, and then many years passed. I attended my thirtieth Hollins reunion, where I was stunned by all our lives. We were divorced; we were gay; we were running large companies; we were living alone on an island; we were dealing with cancer, mental illness, aging parents, children who had not grown up as we'd expected. Some of us had already died, including Mimsy Spieden, who had been on the raft with us. Another woman had simply disappeared. There was a big difference between our youthful expectations and the reality of our lives, between the girls we were then and the women we had become. Suddenly I had plenty of conflict, brought to us by the simple passage of life itself.

Not long after the reunion, a tipsy book club member about my age buttonholed me at a literary festival someplace in the South: "Why do you keep writing about old mountain women?" she demanded. "Why don't you write about us?" Her question hit me with the force of revelation. Okay, I thought, okay. Time to get back on that raft.

SINCE IT'S ALWAYS EASIER FOR me to tell the truth in fiction, *The Last Girls* is a novel. Many of its events are real—luckily I had saved that ship's log, so I knew exactly where and when we had docked all the way down the river, and what happened there. The time the photographer fell in the river trying to take our picture in Arkansas, for instance, or the time that sheriff in Mississippi insisted upon bringing "trusties" from the jail to guard us as we camped—we were all terrified of the trusties, and kept a watch on them ourselves. But we are not the characters of the novel. I made the characters up from scratch, to exemplify various aspects of women's lives that I wanted to talk about. The most important one was Baby—the wild one, the unpredictable one, the catalyst for everything. We have all known somebody like Baby. Conflict follows her around like a puppy dog.

In the novel, a tragedy has brought four of the original "girls," now middle-aged—plus one husband—back together for a repeat voyage under very different circumstances, on the luxurious steamboat *Belle of Natchez*. These women are all carrying a lot of psychological baggage from the past, while dealing with unresolved conflicts in their present lives. In *The Last Girls*,

I'm trying to examine the idea of romance, the relevance of past to present, the themes of memory and desire.

For me—and for most of us on the real raft, I suspect—it was the only journey I ever made that ended as it was supposed to. Subsequent trips have been harder, scarier. We have been shipwrecked, we have foundered on hidden shoals, we have lost our running lights. The captain is dead. I can't stick to a traditional plot anymore. I've got plenty of conflict, plenty of complication, but no resolutions in sight. Such a plot (the heroic quest and conquer) may have been more suited to boys' books anyway. Certainly, the linear, beginning-middle-end form doesn't fit the lives of any women I know. For life has turned out to be wild and various, full of the unexpected, and it's a monstrous big river out here.

On Lou's Porch

IT WAS THE HOT, MUGGY summer of 1980; I was in Abingdon, Virginia, for a week to teach the creative writing class
that always preceded "literary day" at the Virginia Highlands
Festival. I got hotter and hotter each step I took up the long
staircase to the room where the class would meet, above the
sanctuary in the old United Methodist Church right on Main
Street. Finally I made it, and surveyed the group seated around
a big oak table. It was about what you'd expect—eight or ten
people, mostly high school English teachers, some librarians,
some retirees. We had already gone around the table and introduced ourselves when here came this old woman in a man's

hat and fuzzy bedroom shoes, gray head shaking a little with palsy, huffing and puffing up the stairs, dropping notebooks and pencils all over the place, greeting everybody with a smile and a joke. She was a real commotion all by herself.

"Hello there, young lady," she said to me. "My name is Lou Crabtree, and I just love to write!" My heart sank like a stone. Here was every creative writing teacher's nightmare: the nutty old lady who will invariably write sentimental drivel and monopolize the class as well.

"Pleased to meet you," I lied. The week stretched out before me, hot and intolerable, an eternity. But I had to pull myself together. Looking around at all those sweaty, expectant faces, I began, "Okay, now I know you've brought a story with you to read to the group, so let's start out by thinking about beginnings, about how we start a story . . . let's go around the room, and I want you to read the first line of your story aloud."

So we began. Nice lines, nice people. A bee hummed at the open window; a square of golden sunlight fell on the old oak table; somebody somewhere was mowing grass. We got to Lou, who cleared her throat and read this line: "Old Rellar had thirteen miscarriages and she named every one of them."

I sat up. "Would you read that line again?" I asked.

"Old Rellar had thirteen miscarriages and she named every one of them," Lou read.

I took a deep breath. "Keep going," I said.

"Only of late, she got mixed up and missed some. This

bothered her. She looked toward the iron bed. It had always been exactly the same. First came the prayer, then the act with Old Man gratifying himself . . ."

She read the whole thing. It ended with the lines: "You live all your life and work things up to come to nothing. The bull calf bawled somewhere."

I had never heard anything like it.

"Lou," I asked her after class, "have you written anything else? I'd like to see it."

The next day, she brought a battered suitcase. And there it all was, poems and stories written on every conceivable kind of notebook and paper, even old posters and shirtbacks.

Lou grinned at me. "This ain't all, either," she said. The next day, she brought more.

All that week, I read these poems and stories, immersing myself in Lou's magic, primal world of river hills and deep forest, of men and women and children as elemental as nature itself, of talking animals and ghosts, witchcraft and holiness. For Lou Crabtree was that rarity—a writer of perfect pitch and singular knowledge, a real artist. And most amazing of all (to me, anyway, simultaneously revising a mediocre novel of my own), she had written all this with no thought of publication. Writing was how she lived, I realized. It was what she lived by.

"I just write for my own enjoyment," Lou told me. "It pleases me very much to sit down with pencil and paper, and something will come out that looks pretty good, and sounds pretty good, and it gives me pleasure in my soul. I think the best writing time is in the night time. And it is a wonderful time between twelve o'clock and maybe four . . . It is a very strange feeling when all the world is asleep but you. You feel like you're in touch with something special. And then as I write, I don't know what time it is, what day it is. It is that thing of getting out of yourself, of getting out of the world, going out of the world. You feel good, real good. You have none of these problems or hurts or anything. It is something I wish everybody could discover in their work. If they really are doing the thing they like to do, they are able to get out of their self. And it is wonderful. Very wonderful."

I asked her then what she'd do if somebody came along and told her that she couldn't write anymore. "Well, you know, I would just have to sneak!" she said.

For the first time, I began to understand the therapeutic power of language, the importance of the writing process itself. Years later, I would write a novel named *Fair and Tender Ladies* in which my main character writes letters in order to make sense of her life, in much the same way Lou had always written her poems and stories.

But that summer, I put aside the lackluster novel I was working on, and took Lou up on her offer to guide me and my little boys out "adventuring." We climbed down into a cave where Lou swore that Daniel Boone himself had "hid out." We went walking in the woods. She showed them how to make frog houses and pokeberry ink; we all took off our shoes to wade in the creek, then made little plates and cups for fairies from the red clay mud.

"Here, honey," she said, leaning over to pick up a buckeye as we walked back beneath the sunset sky. "Put this in your pocket. It's good luck. And get your head out of them clouds, honey. Pay attention." We went back to sit on her porch, talking to everybody that came by. We had potato chips and Moon Pies for dinner.

I've been trying to pay attention ever since, realizing that writing is not about fame, or even publication. It is not about exalted language, abstract themes, or the escapades of glamorous people. It is about our own real world and our own real lives and understanding what happens to us day by day, it is about playing with children and listening to old people.

THE PASSAGE OF TIME ADDED a special poignancy to Lou's work. In her poem "Smith Creek No. 1," for instance, she told how she "loathed the likes of Smith Creek where I followed my husband to . . . those years of borning five young ones by myself with no doctor and washing for five on a board until four o'clock, until the sun dropped behind Gumm's Hill." Hard times. Yet after the passage of many years, this period took on a beautiful elegaic glow. In "'Smith Creek No. 2 (feeling bad about writing Smith Creek No. 1),'" she is "calling back those years of planting harvesting / Breathing touching among our meanderings / In and out of lives where we pursued / All strange and wonderful things / Down deep into the mysterious dark / Where the roots wind about the heart" as "The seasons change and go. The fire eyes of an opossum glow." The final image was one of peaceful beauty, life come gloriously full circle at last: "In Smith Creek, a scarlet leaf floats round and round."

"You know how the mist comes up and covers the land, lots of times?" Lou asked me. "Some of these people that I write about are from a long time ago, they're not anymore, they're just kind of like the mist that covers my mountains. Sometimes I think they may still be there in those mountains. My people may still be right there."

Lou was born on the North Fork of the Holston River, one of ten children in the Price family. "We ran all over the hills and watched from behind trees and played Indians, and I knew more flowers and animals than I did people." She went to the Radford Normal School at sixteen, graduating cum laude in three years, then returned home to teach. Lou married Homer Crabtree in 1942 and moved to the Smith Creek area, near where she was born. She had five children in seven years, taking a ten-year leave from teaching to "raise cattle, tobacco, and young'uns. Oh, money is scarce on a mountain." Lou characterized her husband as a "very soft-spoken man . . . a very calm and kind man . . . a man that people would come and sit down and talk to." Later she returned to the classroom, teaching just about every subject at every level, from a one-room school to elementary and high schools.

After Homer's death, Lou bought her home at 313 Valley Street for $4,000, money she'd "saved up" from teaching, and moved into town in 1960 as a widow with five teenagers. In reminiscing about the "early widow phase," Lou winks at me: "Oh, you'll have lots of opportunities as a young widow. They say, 'When you're old, I'll take care of you' . . . like hell they will! I was through and done with all that." Her son George "who raises those old Charolais cattle" shared her Valley Street home for a long time. Even after her official retirement, Lou continued to teach all manner of classes, especially enjoying the GED and English as a Second Language groups, "getting to know some gorgeous people, from Viet Nam, and Japan, and Venezuela . . . well, everyplace!"

She was also the leader of the Rock of Ages Band of senior citizens, which performed all over the area. "We have three pianists in case one gets sick, we can fall back on another one. We have a mandolin player and a guitar player and an autoharp. Mr. Harold Clark on the mandolin, he is eighty-some years old, and he can play that 'Somewhere My Love.' His wife is one of our chaperones. You wouldn't think we need chaperones, but we do! We have got the best banjo player in town, her name is Love Craig, and she is eighty-five years old. Oh, can she play that banjo! Now that is really something, to hear Love Craig play the banjo."

I agree, having served as "roadie" on several tours with the Rock of Ages Band.

But always, Lou was writing, her life a testament to the sustaining and revitalizing power of language. She often stuck her brother into a story. "He died at the age of thirty, after coming back from the war one year, and he was an alcoholic, so that was a great grief to me. Oh yes, we were close. Now once in a while when I put in this character Bud, that's my brother. It makes me feel good, you know, that though he died, I can keep him going." Her writing was widely published; Louisiana State University Press brought out her collection of stories, *Sweet Hollow*, in 1984. (The publisher was startled when he first called her house and George answered, as he invariably did, "Hello! Poorhouse!"—"Hoping they'd think it was something else, and sometimes they did!" Lou laughed.) Her book of poems, *The River Hills and Beyond*, came out from Sow's Ear Press in 1998. Lou won the Virginia Cultural Laureate in Literature Award, the Governor's Award for Arts in Virginia, as well as a special award from the Virginia Highlands Festival. *Calling on Lou,* a one-woman stage play celebrating her life and work, premiered at the Barter Theater in Abingdon and then toured Virginia; she even appeared on the *Today Show*.

But none of this meant much to Lou. She called the later phase of her life "the porch years" and what she liked to do most was sit out on that porch where I visited her so many times amid the jumble of old furniture and plants and knickknacks, just talking and reading and watching the traffic pass by. Sometimes we sang a little. "Oh darling, you can't love but one. Oh darling, you can't love but one. You can't love but one and have any fun . . . You can't love ten and love me again—Oh boy, I'm leaving on that midnight train!" or "Cindy got religion, she danced around and 'round, she got so full of glory, she knocked the preacher down!" We laughed a lot.

In winter, we'd sit inside by the heater near her sturdy bed layered with quilts, books, and manuscripts piled everyplace. Everything in that room was precious to her. "Now, take these cabinets. My husband's people were cabinetmakers. Fine old cabinetmakers. They could join up two pieces of wood so it looked like it growed together. That's my mother's blue vase up there. It is a cobalt blue and they don't make that cobalt anymore. They use all that cobalt in cancer treatment." Lou herself never took so much as an aspirin. She lived entirely in the front room by then, with kitchen and bathroom at hand and a good view of Valley Street out the bay window. She had a steady stream of visitors, pilgrims like myself.

"Why, there've been people here from the Arctic regions, just dying to talk. A man was in here the other day that had climbed Mt. Everest, and a woman came who was going on the Trans-Siberian Railroad. I've always wanted to go on that myself," Lou told me.

"Why not?" I asked. "A lot of people take up traveling when they retire."

"Why, I don't have to!" she laughed. "I have traveled all over the world right here on this porch. People talk to me, they take me to all these places that they've been to. We are in a changing time, but people do like to talk. They will come and sit down here and talk—especially if they can laugh!"

"These porch years are very creative for me," Lou said. She also called them her "spiritual years." She became interested in space, even taking a course from the University of Virginia. She wrote more than fifty "space poems."

When I asked why she had gotten so fascinated with space, Lou answered, "Because it's out there! Our universe is like a great big clock, run by God's laws of chemistry, math, biology, and science . . . Now you know He doesn't do things mishmash! And there'll come a day when the spirit will take leave of this old body. It's going to rise up to Paradise, and I wanted to know where Paradise was! So I've found out by science how it's going to happen. When you go faster than the speed of light, then you get younger and younger. Science and scripture agree! You're going to live forever in paradise, and you'll be young. I can't wait!"

Lou's new interest seemed to be an expansion—not a contradiction—of traditional religion. "I went to churches all my life," she told me, mentioning the old Centenary Methodist Church in particular. "I never went to a church in my life that I wasn't helped. And now," she said, "I'm open! I'm open to everything!"

I told Lou that I believed I finally understand something she told me so long ago: "'You have to travel a lonely road. It is you yourself traveling along, and if you are able along the road to meet a friend, to meet a love . . . you're very, very lucky. But it is a lonely road even though you have sons and daughters that you love better than your own life—that you'd give your own life for. One day you have to let them go, you let them all go. Oh, all right, it's a lonely road.'"

Now I know what she meant.

"Do you ever have times you can't sleep?" she asked me. "You probably don't, but you will, honey, you will. Well, things will rise out of the night, some way or other. All our people back of us can rise and come out in the night time awful good, and talk to us, and comfort us. Why I saw your mother one time, Lee, sitting in a rocking chair on the porch of the Martha Washington Inn! I saw your pa driving that fancy car right up to heaven.

"Death should be thought of as a beautiful part of life," Lou said. "I'm not a bit afraid of dying. I want to die right here in this old bed with a pencil in my hand." But not anytime soon—"I want to make it to 2000. I'd like to see what they do and say about it!"

Actually she made it to April 10, 2006, dying in her sleep at ninety-three. I had promised Lou I would "preach at her funeral" and I did—one of several speakers at the same Abingdon United Methodist Church where we had first met in the creative writing class, all those years ago. I read her poem "Salvation" aloud at the service. Afterward I walked over to Valley Street and stood for a long time looking at Lou's house, which had been sold and spruced up. The porch looked like anybody's porch now. I remembered her words, "We are all going in a circle, and death is not the end of our circle. It is just a word that some people have." I fingered the buckeye in my pocket.

LOU'S POEM "SALVATION" WAS printed in the program for her funeral on April 14, 2006.

SALVATION

jesus jesus jesus i got something
     this old body aint so important
in this old body i feel holiness i got holiness
     i got jesus flirtin with death

ever day in the coal mines flirtin with death
my daddy flirted and my brothers flirted
     and my uncles and cousins
and my daddy got his back broken
     flirtin with death

brother flirtin with death motorcycles, race cars
     not my way flirtin with death
sister flirted i danced around her coffin
     high in my hand same snake caused her death

laid her three weeks baby in her dead arms
sister got holiness flirtin with death

i feel holiness jesus i got something
washing the feet laying on hands dancing the fire dance
      glory glory glory
praying for the sign the wounded blood of jesus
   on the feet on the hands on the head
praying three years for the jesus sign
      glory hallelujah

in the church house old snake washed clean
i put him to my shoulder flirtin with death
i touch him to my lips flirtin with death
flirtin with death i raise him to my breast
old velvet lips with his singing tail and lightning breath
i offer old velvet lips my snowy white breast

jesus jesus this old body aint so important
i got holiness flirtin with death

—Lou V. Price Crabtree
(March 13, 1913–April 10, 2006)

Lightning Storm

WHEN I WAS A CHILD, books brought my deepest pleasure, my greatest excitement. Reading, I often felt exactly the way I felt during summer thunderstorms: I just had to run out of the house and up the mountain into the very storm to whirl in the thunder and rain on the rocky top while lightning cracked all around me.

Since the next best thing to reading books was writing them and talking about them, I ended up becoming a writer and a professor. But then there came a time when I realized that I was hearing entirely too much about agents and advances, about "revising the canon" and "privileging the text" and "writing across the curriculum." I became depressed about writing, which no longer seemed relevant to anything real. I had lost the lightning.

So when a Lila Wallace–Readers' Digest Writers' Award in 1992 offered me the chance to get out of my college classroom and affiliate with a nonprofit group of my choice for some community involvement, I jumped at the chance to get back to the coal fields.

I chose to work with the Hindman Settlement School in Hindman, Kentucky. I had often been a visiting writer for their summer creative writing workshop. The school's adult learning center, a no-nonsense brick building overhanging a muddy creek, offered a year-round literacy program, adult education classes, and tutoring services for the high school equivalency exam. The need for these programs is great. Half the county's population hasn't made it through high school; most dropouts leave before the ninth grade. Unemployment is high, and incomes are low.

I had the privilege of visiting this ongoing program each fall and spring for three years. At the Settlement School, I lived in a log house, gave readings and talks at area schools and community colleges, and conducted several daily workshops with students in the programs at the Adult Learning Center. We usually had ten to eighteen people per group; I also worked one-on-one with several people who really had a lot to say—some began writing their own life stories.

Since I can't actually remember the time when I couldn't read and write, I didn't understand the enormous sense of empowerment that comes with mastering written language. It was a revelation for me to meet red-headed, good-looking Connel Polly of Vicco, Kentucky, a successful grading contractor who had kept his illiteracy secret from everybody but his wife for fifty years. In *It's Like Coming Out of a Deep Hole*, his booklet of memories printed by the Hindman School, he recounts this incident:

> One time, the mining company sent me to Canton, Ohio, going after mine parts in a pickup truck. They had told me which roads to take and what the exit was, and I was supposed to find this company that was on Fifth Street. So I drove all around looking for a five, and I couldn't find it. That's when I realized "Fifth" was a word, and I couldn't read it. I couldn't find it. That's the only time I ever cried in my life. I just pulled off the road and sat there and cried. I was eight hours away from home and it was getting dark. That was pitiful. Finally I had to ask somebody, and it turned out I was sitting right at it. I could see it. I felt so bad I didn't even stay the night. After I did my business I drove on back, and I was down all the way home. I was so blue. I felt the worst I've ever felt. There I was—a grown man—trying to make a living in that shape!

Now, he writes:

> I didn't know learning to read would change my life so much. It has made me have more confidence in myself. Before, I even had a fear of going into a public restroom. I had fear of being embarrassed by someone handing me something to read. I

stayed away from places such as banks, post offices, and doctors' offices. The first visit to a new doctor was hardest because you had to fill out forms. I always had my wife with me. Now, I'll go anywhere. Also, me and my wife leave notes for each other. Now that's something!

Lively Florida Slone, a well-known local ballad singer, did not enroll until the death of her husband. She writes:

I always thought of myself as a bean planted in a garden, and then someone put a big rock on top of me so that I could not get out of the ground. Now . . . I have gotten my driver's license, and I can write my own checks. I can read my Bible and my songbooks. I have always liked to make up songs and stories, but I never could write them down before. Now I can. I am beginning to grow. Maybe one of these days I'll be like Jack's beanstalk!

Mrs. Slone became a participant in many activities at the Adult Learning Center, where her outgoing personality brought her many friends.

The school put together a collection of Mrs. Slone's writing entitled *A Garden of Songs*, which range from love songs to hymns ("Voice of Angels"); to funny party tunes like "Chew Tobacco" and "Big Fat Dog." There are also story songs such as "Red Hot Election" and "School Bus Wreck in Floyd County" that chronicle local events.

She tells the circumstances that occasioned the writing of each song. "One time I was asked to leave a church because my husband had been married before—they called him 'a old double-married thing.' I went home and wrote this song. I wrote it to give me comfort. I wanted the world to know that Jesus was the pastor in my church, not somebody else." That song is entitled "To All the People Looking Down Their Nose at Me."

Some of Mrs. Slone's songs are pure poetry. About the composition of "Last Night," she tells us, "It was rainy one night, and the clouds were passing by, and I could hear the whippoorwills calling—it's been years ago."

Last night I sat and watched the clouds go by
I heard whippoorwills call from the mountains so high
I heard the water as it dropped soft and low
Seems like death is a secret nobody knows.

Other writers also took the opportunity to express deep feelings. Pretty young Promise Sandling wrote about her childhood:

I used to feel like no one loved me cause
My family was always falling apart
All my dads always left
But now I feel wonderful-N-I am happy
Because guess what?
I think I am smart!

Most of my writing students were women. Some had been unable go to school when they were girls because of early pregnancies; local churches and general opinion were against abortion, so this had not been an option. Married or not, these women had raised their children, often in difficult circumstances. Other girls had needed to stay home from school to help out with younger children or sick family members. Many enrolled upon discovering, after divorce or widowhood, what they could do for themselves.

Glenda Johnson, who eventually had to drop out of the program to tend ailing relatives, first found the time to write about her son:

This is a poem about Roy Glen Johnson.

He lives in a wooden house
At Mallie, KY 41836
He has blue eyes
and blond looking hair and
he likes to ride his bike.
He likes to play outside all the time.
He is afraid of my father.
He would like to have
His family whole again.

When I first visited the high school equivalency program, black-haired, statuesque Ollie Wallen had just enrolled. She looked down all the time, and didn't say much. Two years later,

Ollie was wearing nail polish and joining vigorously in every discussion. She wrote to her congressman with a complaint and was pleased when he called her at home to advise her how to take action on getting benefits she was due. Here is a poem by Ollie:

I used to be married
But now I am divorced.
I used to do things for my husband
But now I do things for myself.
I used to feel bad about myself,
But now I feel great about myself,
Like a rope was wrapped around me
But now it is loose.

It's a long, winding road from where I am living now to the mountains of eastern Kentucky. But it brought me home. My involvement with this program made me remember what reading and writing were all about in the first place, before book tours and disputes about deconstructionism. Helping people express themselves in writing for the first time is like watching them fall in love. For me, it brought back the old thrill, the lightning storm.

Driving Miss Daisy Crazy; or, Losing the Mind of the South

I want to start by introducing you to Miss Daisy. Chances are, you already know her. She may be your mother. She may be your aunt. Or you may have your own private Miss Daisy, as I do: a prim, well-educated maiden lady of a certain age who has taken up permanent residence in a neat little room in the frontal lobe of my brain. I wish she'd move, but as she points out to me constantly, she's just no trouble at all. She lives on angel food cake and she-crab soup, which she heats up on a little ring right there in her room.

Miss Daisy was an English teacher at a private girls' school for forty-three years, back in the days when English was English—before it became Language Arts. She was famous for her ability to diagram sentences, any sentence at all, even sentences so complex that their diagrams on the board looked like blueprints for a cathedral. Her favorite poet is Sidney Lanier. She likes to be elevated. She is still in a book club, but it is not Oprah's book club. In fact, Miss Daisy is not quite sure who Oprah is, believing that her name is Okra Winfrey, and asking me repeatedly what all the fuss is about. Miss Daisy's book club can find scarcely a thing to elevate them these days, so they have taken to reading *Gone With the Wind* over and over again.

Miss Daisy's favorite word is *ought*, as in "You ought to go to church this morning." She often punctuates her sentences with "you know," as in, "Lee Marshall, you know you don't believe that!" or, "Lee Marshall, you know you don't mean it!" She believes it is true about the two ladies who got kicked out of the Nashville Junior League: one for having an orgasm, and the other for having a job.

In fact, Miss Daisy reminds me of another lady I encountered many years ago, when I moved down to Alabama to become a reporter for *The Tuscaloosa News*. The former editor of the ladies page of the paper had just retired. "Thank God!" everybody said, since for many years she had ceased to write up events in the paper the way they actually happened, preferring instead to write them up the way she thought they should have happened.

The South runs on denial. We learn denial in the cradle and carry it to the grave. It is absolutely essential to being a lady, for instance. My Aunt Gay-Gay's two specialties were Rising to the Occasion and Rising Above It All, whatever "it" happened to be. Aunt Gay-Gay believed that if you can't say something nice, say nothing at all. If you don't discuss something, it doesn't exist. She drank a lot of gin and tonics and sometimes she'd start in on them early, winking at my Uncle Bob and saying, "Pour me one, honey, it's already dark underneath the house." Until she died, I never knew that another of my aunts had had a previous marriage. It had been edited right out of the family, in the same way all pictures of that husband had been removed from the family albums.

Denial affects not only our personal lives, but also our political lives, our culture, and our literature. In her book *Playing in the Dark: Whiteness and the Literary Imagination*, Toni Morrison talks about a kind of denial she sees operating in American literature and criticism; she chides liberal critics for what she calls their "neglect of darkness." She says that "the habit of ignoring race is understood to be a graceful, even generous, liberal gesture . . . but excising the political from the life of the mind is a sacrifice that has proven costly. . . . A criticism that needs to insist that literature is not only 'universal' but also 'race-free' risks lobotomizing that literature, and diminishes both the art and the artist." Morrison suggests that black characters in classic American novels have been as marginalized as their real-life counterparts.

But back to Miss Daisy. I'm taking her out to lunch today. Miss Daisy claims she "just eats like a bird," not deigning to confess to anything as base as hunger or even appetite, but she does like to go out to lunch. And while she's making her final preparations—that is, clean underwear in case we are in a wreck, gloves, money safely tucked in her bra in case her purse is stolen—let me tell you about this restaurant we're going to.

You may be surprised to learn that I actually own this restaurant, and that it is actually a sushi bar. But, hey! It's the New South, remember? And actually, our sushi bar (named Akai Hana and located in Carrboro, North Carolina) presents a little case study in the New South.

The land Akai Hana stands on today, at 206 W. Main St, was farmland not so very long ago, when Carrboro was a dusty, sleepy little farm village on the old road from Chapel Hill to Greensboro. This was an open field, with a tenant house at the end of it. Then Carr Mill came in, and mill houses sprouted up in neat little rows, like beans, to house the families that worked at Carr Mill. As the university grew, Chapel Hill grew, too, spreading outward toward Carrboro, which gradually became a service adjunct of Chapel Hill. This was the place you came to buy your grass seed or to get your tires fixed at the Chapel Hill Tire Company, right across the street from us. Carrboro was mostly black then, and all poor. Miss Daisy never came here except to pick up her cook. Every business in Carrboro closed at noon on Wednesday, because everybody went to church on Wednesday night. And nothing was open on Sunday.

Our brick building, constructed in the early fifties, was first occupied by a popular, locally owned café named the Elite

Lunch, which featured Southern cooking and lots of it. It had two dining rooms, one for white and one for colored. In the early sixties it was superseded by Pizza Villa, whose name alone testifies to Chapel Hill's—and Carrboro's—increasing sophistication. By now, plenty of graduate students and even some professors lived in Carrboro. The mill had closed, and those mill houses were affordable.

By the mid-seventies, when an outrageously colorful chef took over and turned it into Avanti, Carrboro was coming of age. The mill became Carr Mill Mall, filled with trendy boutiques. In the eighties, a cooperative health-food grocery named Weaver Street Market opened up. Artists moved in. Carrboro started calling itself the Paris of the Piedmont.

Avanti's chef hung paintings by his artist friends. He stuck candles in wine bottles on each of his artfully mismatched tables. He opened the patio for outdoor dining. He made soup with forty cloves of garlic. Then, even Avanti was superseded by the truly gourmet Martini's. The owner's wife's mother came from Italy to run the kitchen, while her homemade pasta dried on broomsticks upstairs. My first husband and I had some memorable meals there, and my present husband remembers that he was eating polenta in this very gazebo when a former girlfriend gave him the gate. Ah, what sweet revenge it is now to own that gazebo, which we have (of course) transformed into a pagoda.

But back to our narrative. The owner died in a wreck,

Martini's closed, and the restaurant underwent a total transformation before opening again, for breakfast and lunch only, as a bakery and café, very French, with a marble floor and lace curtains at the windows. Pre-Starbucks, the two ladies who now owned it served muffins accompanied by the first good coffee in Carrboro.

We bought the place from the muffin ladies. Why? You might well ask. Have I always had a burning desire to go into the sushi business? No, actually, my own attitude toward raw fish is closer to Roy Blount's poem about oysters:

> I prefer my oyster fried.
> Then I'm sure my oyster's died.

IT WAS MY HUSBAND'S IDEA. He always called my son Josh the "samurai stepson," and their favorite thing to do together was to go out for sushi. The closing of the only sushi bar in town coincided with Josh's improvement from schizophrenia. New medications made it possible for him to have a more regular life, and what better job could a samurai stepson get than in a sushi bar? (I can hear Miss Daisy saying in my ear, "Now Lee Marshall, you know you shouldn't have told that!" But I am telling it anyway.) We held long conferences with Bob, the sushi chef. We met with the muffin ladies and the bank. We hired a designer and a construction firm. We were under way, even though nobody except us thought this was a good idea. Our accountant was horrified. The guys from the tire shop across the street kept coming over to ask, "How's the bait shop coming along?"

We opened in 1997. Let me introduce you around.

Bob, manager and head chef, hails from the coastal North Carolina town of Swansboro. At college in Chapel Hill, he wrote poetry and played guitar until his wanderlust led him to California, where he eventually became an ardent convert of the Reverend Moon and joined the Unification Church. He married his Japanese wife, Ryoko, in a ceremony of twenty-five thousand couples in Madison Square Garden. They are still happily married, with six beautiful children.

Under Bob's direction, Akai Hana employs people from diverse backgrounds, including Hispanic, Burmese, Thai, Japanese, Filipino, Chinese, Korean, African-American, and African. Meet Rick, for instance, who heads the kitchen in back (yes, we do have cooked food, for people like Miss Daisy, who is enjoying some grilled teriyaki chicken right now). Anyway, both Rick and his wife, a beautician, are Chinese Filipinos who have been in this country for eighteen years, sending for their siblings one by one. Their son, a physician, is now completing his residency in Seattle. Their daughter, who recently earned her doctorate in public health, works for a world health organization in L.A. Rick's nephew Brian, one of the wait staff, plays saxophone in the UNC jazz band.

Ye-tun, a cook and a former Burmese freedom fighter whose

nickname is "Yel," proudly showed me a picture of himself coming through the jungle dressed in camo, carrying an AK-47. Now my husband calls him the "Rebel Yell," but nobody gets it.

Okay: Bob, Ryoko, Brian, Helen Choi, Ye-tun, Miguel, Jose, Genita, Mister Chiba, and Mister Choi—these people are Southerners. We are all Southerners. Akai Hana is a Southern restaurant, just like Pittypat's Porch or Hardee's.

Judging merely from our lunch at Akai Hana, we are going to have to seriously overhaul our image of the South, and of Southerners, for this millennium.

My little piece of land in Carrboro is typical. The South was two-thirds rural in the 1930s. Now it is over two-thirds urban. One half of all Southerners were farmworkers in the thirties; now that statistic is at 2 percent. And out of those farmworkers in the thirties, one half were tenant farmers. Now we have no tenant farmers, but migrant workers instead.

Our Southern birthrate, which used to be famously above the national average, is now below it. This means that immigration—and in-migration—are defining the South's population. Soon Texas and Florida will both have nonwhite majorities.

Well, this very idea has given Miss Daisy a headache. She just doesn't have a head for figures, anyway. She'd like some dessert, but Akai Hana serves only green tea ice cream, which is too weird to even think about, in Miss Daisy's opinion. So we pay up and drive a few blocks down to Mama Dip's Country Kitchen, where Mildred "Dip" Council, Miss Daisy's former cook, has opened her big, fancy new restaurant. She's published a cookbook, too. She's been written up by Calvin Trillin and Craig Claiborne; she's been on TV. She's an entrepreneur now. Miss Daisy orders the lemon chess pie. I go for the peach cobbler myself.

Some things never change. Some Southern food will never go out of style, no matter how much it may get nouveau'ed. And large parts of the South still look a lot like they used to—the Appalachian coal country where I'm from, for instance, and the old Cotton Belt. A layer of cultural conservatism still covers Dixie like the dew. As a whole, we Southerners are still religious, and we are still violent. We'll bring you a casserole, but we'll kill you, too. Southern women, both black and white, have always been more likely than Northern women to work outside the home, despite the image projected by such country lyrics as "Get your biscuits in the oven and your buns in the bed, this women's liberation is a-going to your head." It was not because we were so liberated; it's because we were so poor. This, too, is changing: now our per capita income is at 92 percent of the national average.

With all these changes, what should I tell my student, one of my very favorite students, who burst into tears after we attended a reading together at which Elizabeth Spencer read her fine short story "The Cousins." "I'll never be a Southern writer!" my student wailed. "I don't even know my cousins!" Raised in a military household, relocated many times, she had absolutely no sense of place, no sense of the past, no sense of family. How did she spend her childhood? I asked. In the mall in Fayetteville, North Carolina, she tearfully confessed, sneaking cigarettes and drinking Cokes.

I told her she was lucky.

But she was also right. For a writer cannot pick her material any more than she can pick her parents; her material is given to her by circumstances of her birth, by how she first hears language. And if she happens to be Southern, these factors may already be trite, even before she sits down at her computer to begin. Her neurasthenic, fragile Aunt Lena is already trite, her mean, scary cousin Bobby Lee is already trite, her columned, shuttered house in Natchez is already trite. Far better to start out from the mall in Fayetteville, illicit cigarette in hand, with no cousins to hold her back, and venture forth fearlessly into the New South.

I once heard the novelist George Garrett say that the House of Fiction has many rooms. Well, the House of Southern Fiction is in the process of remodeling. It needs so many more rooms that we've got brand-new wings shooting out from the main house in every direction. It looks like one of those pictures of the sun as drawn by a second-grader. In fact, that's the name of it—the House of the Rising Sun—which is right over here by the interstate. I'll run you by it as we drive Miss Daisy home.

Look—there's my student right now, knocking on the door,

suitcase in hand. She doesn't know yet that once she takes a room in there, she can never come out again. She doesn't understand that she's giving up her family and her home forever, that as soon as she writes about those things she will lose them, in a way, though she will mythologize them in her work, the way we all do, with all our little hometowns of the heart.

Allan Gurganus has called ours "the literature of nostalgia," pointing out that many of the great anthems of the South are written from a position of exile such as "Way down upon the Swanee River"; "I wish I was in the land of cotton"; James Taylor's "going to Carolina in my mind"; or "Country roads, take me home."

The writer puts herself in exile by the very act of writing. She will feel guilty about leaving, and for the rest of her life, she will write, in part, to expunge this guilt. Back home, they will be embarrassed by what she's become, wishing that she'd married well and joined the country club instead. Mostly, they just won't mention it, sticking to safer subjects.

Miss Daisy and I sit in the car watching my student, who keeps banging on the door, trying to get in there. "Honey, don't do it!" Miss Daisy rolls down her window and cries across the grass. "Go back home! It's not too late to stop!" But of course it is. Now my student is trying to peer in a window, shading her eyes with her hand.

Oh, I remember when I was that age myself, desperate for a room in the House of the Rising Sun. You think you'll pay for it out of your day job, and maybe you will for a while, but you'll whore out, too, eventually. We all do. The House of the Rising Sun is full of desperate characters. Some of us are drinking ourselves to death quietly, in our rooms, or loudly, at MLA. A lot of us are involved in secret affairs and unseemly couplings—we'd be real embarrassed if everybody knew who we're sleeping with. Some of us just can't do it anymore, but we put on our makeup anyway, and sit at the window all dressed up, and talk about doing it.

Look! The door is opening, just a crack. It's the Madam herself, but she stands just far enough back in the shadows so you can't really see who she is—maybe it's Shannon Ravenel, or maybe it's Okra.

My student slips inside. She does not look back.

"Well, I never!" Miss Daisy announces before falling over into a dead faint on the seat beside me.

But I know she'll be all right. I know she'll be herself again by the time I get her back to her room, and she'll be talking about what's happened to my student, and she'll make a big story out of it, and she will never, ever, shut up.

This is the main thing that has not changed about the South, in my opinion—that will never change. We Southerners love a story, and we will tell you anything.

Just look at Miss Daisy now. She's already sitting back up on the seat fanning herself and going on and on about what happened to that poor girl, which reminds her of another awful thing that happened to her niece Margaret's daughter, not the Margaret I know that lives in Atlanta, but the other one that lives in middle Tennessee who was never quite right in the head after that terrible automobile accident that happened when she was not but six when Cousin Dan was driving in that open car, you know he was such an alcoholic . . .

Good-bye to the Sunset Man

KEY WEST, FLORIDA — JANUARY 29, 2004

Once again my husband and I line up for sunset cruise tickets on the tall vintage schooner *Western Union*, which sways in its dock here at the end of William Street, here at the end of America.

"How many?" The handsome blonde in the ticket booth looks like she used to be a man.

"Three," I say.

"Two," Hal says, turning around to look at me.

"So how many is it?" She drums her long nails on the wooden counter.

"Two," Hal says. He gives her his credit card.

She slides over two tickets for the sunset cruise and two coupons for free drinks, which we order on the roof of the

Schooner Wharf Bar where we wait until time to board. This year we are here without my son, Josh, who died in his sleep this past October 26. The cause of his death was an "acute myocardiopathy," the collapse of an enlarged heart brought about, in part, I believe, by all the weight he had gained while taking an antipsychotic drug. He was thirty-three; he had been sick for half his life, doing daily heroic battle with the brain disorder that first struck while he was in a program for gifted teen musicians at the Berklee College of Music in Boston, the summer between his junior and senior years in high school.

Back in Chapel Hill, we'd started getting wilder and wilder phone calls from him about "birds flying too close to the sun," reports of all-night practice sessions on the piano, strange encounters in the park, and no sleep—no sleep, ever. He flew home in a straitjacket.

Then the hospitalizations began—first a lengthy stay at Holly Hill in Raleigh, followed by a short, heartbreaking try at returning home to normalcy and Chapel Hill High; then long-term care at Highland Hospital in Asheville, where he lived for the next four years, sometimes in the hospital itself, sometimes in their group home, sometimes in an apartment with participation in their day program. For a while he was better, then not. All kinds of fantasies and scenarios rolled through his head. He moved, talked, and dressed bizarrely; he couldn't remember anything; he couldn't even read. We brought him back to the University of North Carolina's Neurosciences Hospital. They referred him to Dorothea Dix's test program for the recently approved "wonder drug" clozapine.

Up on that beautiful, windy hill looking out over the city of Raleigh, Josh started getting truly better for the first time. He could participate in a real conversation; he could make a joke. It was literally a miracle.

He was able to leave the hospital and enter Caramore Community in Chapel Hill, which offered vocational rehabilitation, a group home, and then a supervised apartment—as well as a lot of camaraderie. He came by with some great stories as he worked with the Caramore lawn and housecleaning business. Once, the housecleaning crew dared one of the gang to jump into the baptismal pool at a local church they were cleaning— and then they all "baptized" him on the spot. Before long, Josh graduated into a real job, at Carolina Cleaners. Against all odds, Josh had become a "working man," as he always referred to himself; his pride in this was enormous.

Though other hospitalizations ("tune-ups," he called them) would be required from time to time, Josh was on his way. He lived in his own apartment, drove a car, managed his weekly doctor visits, blood tests, pharmacy trips and medication. But as the most important part of his own "treatment team," he steadfastly refused his doctor's eventual urging to switch to one of the newer drugs, such as olanzapine, risperidone, or geodon, in hopes of jump-starting his metabolism. Clozapine had given him back his life, and he didn't want to give it up. And in spite of his weight and smoking, he seemed healthy enough; physical examinations didn't ring any warning bells.

Josh became a familiar figure in Chapel Hill and Carrboro, with friends and acquaintances all over town—especially his regular haunts such as Weaver Street Market and Caffé Driade, where he went every day. Josh worked at Akai Hana for the last seven years of his life, doing everything from washing dishes to prep work to lunchtime sushi chef. He was the first one there every morning—he opened up and started preparing the rice. It was his favorite time of the day, as he often said. He played piano there every Saturday night: a mix of jazz, blues, and his own compositions. He put together a tape that he named *Five Not So Easy Pieces*.

The live music produced by the Wharf Bar's Jimmy Buffett wannabe band is way too loud, and our drinks, when they come, are a startling shade of red, with umbrellas in them. Hal raises his plastic glass high. "Here's to the big guy," he says. We drain them.

Josh considered the schooner trip a requisite for his annual Key West experience. He loved the ritual of it all, beginning when the crew invited the evening's passengers to participate in raising the mainsail. He always went over to line up and pull, passing the halyard hand over hand to the next guy. He loved to stand at the rail as we passed the town dock and Mallory Square, where all the weird pageantry of the sunset was already in full swing: the tourists, the guy with the trained housecats, the flame swallower, the escape artist tied up in chains, the oddly menacing cookie lady. The aging hippie musician on board invariably cranked up "Sloop John B" as we headed out to sea while the sun sank lower on the starboard side. I remember on our last trip together, the sun was so bright that I couldn't even face it without sunglasses, but Josh didn't wear them. He just sat there perfectly still, staring straight into the sun, a little smile playing around his lips.

What thoughts went through his head on that last voyage?

Perhaps more to the point, what thoughts did not go through his head, in this later stage of schizophrenia characterized by "blank mind" and "lack of affect"? Gone were the voices, gone the visions, gone the colored lights, to be replaced by . . . what? Maybe nothing, like the bodhisattva, a person who has achieved the final apotheosis, beyond desire and self. Here he sat, an immense man in a black T-shirt and blue jeans, silent, calm, apparently at peace. He no longer seemed to know what he had lost. Some call this a "blessing," and some days I am among them; but most days I am not, remembering instead that wild boy of seventeen who wanted the world—all the music; all the friends, BMX bikes and skateboards; all the poetry; all the girls—all the life there ever was.

Now the captain is blowing the conch shell from the deck of the *Western Union*. We stand. The sun slants into our eyes. A breeze is coming up. I pull on my windbreaker, fingering the little bronze vial of ashes in my pocket.

It's time.

The previous January Josh and I had flown into Key West together, arriving around 9 p.m. on a cool and blustery Tuesday night. Wind rattled the palm fronds as we walked out onto the brightly lit but somehow lonely-looking Duval Street. Only a few people scurried past, their shoulders hunched against the wind. We passed the Chicken Store, a "safe house" for the much-maligned chickens that have overrun Key West. We passed the Scrub Club, an "adult" bathhouse that usually featured its scantily clad ladies blowing bubbles over the balcony rail, calling out, "Hi there! Feeling dirty? Need a bath?" to the amused passersby. But it was too cool for bubbles that night, and the girls were all inside behind their red door. The wind whipped paper trash along the street.

We crossed Duval and went into the friendly-looking Original Coffee and Tea House. Big trees overhung the old bungalow, its porch and yard filled with comfortable, mismatched furniture. Josh was very tired. He had that blank look he sometimes got, almost vegetative, like a big sweet potato. We walked up the concrete steps and into the bar, with its comforting, helpful smell of coffee brewing. People clustered at little tables, on sofas, in armchairs in adjacent rooms, talking and reading the newspapers strewn everyplace.

The bartender's long, gray hair was pulled back into a ponytail. He came over to Josh and said, "What can I get for you, sir?"

"Well, I'll tell you," Josh said in a surprisingly loud voice (maybe it even surprised him), shaking his head like a dog coming up from under the water. "I'll tell you, buddy, I don't know what the hell it is I want, and I don't know where the hell it is I am, and I don't know what the hell it is I'm doing!"

Heads along the bar swiveled, and the bartender burst out laughing. "In that case, sir, you've come to the right island!" he announced, as everybody applauded.

Josh had found his Key West home for the next week. At bars or beaches, he talked to everybody; you never knew what he was going to say next.

He told a great version of the Christmas story, too, conflating the Bible with O. Henry: "Once upon a time there was a young girl who was very sick, and somehow she got the idea that she would die when all the leaves fell off the tree that grew just outside her bedroom window. One by one they dropped. She got sicker and sicker. Finally there was only one red leaf left on the tree; she was just about to die. That night while she was asleep, Jesus flew up to her window. Jesus was a French artist. He wore a red beret. So he brought his box of oil paints with him and painted red leaves all over the window, finishing just as the sun came up and the last red leaf fluttered down to the ground. Then he flew away. Then she woke up, and she was well, and it was Christmas."

I asked him whether or not he believed in Jesus. "Well, I don't know," he said. "Every time I'm in the hospital, there are at least three people in there who think they're Jesus. So sometimes I think, well, maybe Jesus wasn't Jesus at all—maybe he was just the first schizophrenic."

Josh's eventual diagnosis was schizoaffective disorder, meaning partly schizophrenic (his mind did not work logically, his senses were often unreliable, his grip on reality sometimes tenuous) and partly bipolar—actually a blessing, since the characteristic "ups and downs" allowed him more expression and empathy. But psychiatric diagnosis is tricky at best. The sudden onset of these major brain disorders usually occurs in the late teens or early twenties, and it's usually severe. However all psychosis looks alike at first. There's no way to distinguish between the "highs" of bipolar illness, for instance, and the florid stage of schizophrenia—or even a garden-variety LSD psychosis. Reality has fled in every case. The best doctors make no claims; "Wait and see," they say.

As far as prognosis goes, medical folklore holds to a "rule of three": About a third of all people with major psychotic episodes will actually get well, such as Kurt Vonnegut's son, Mark, now a physician, who wrote the memoir *The Eden Express*. The next, larger group will be in and out of hospitals and programs for the rest of their lives, with wildly varying degrees of success in work and life situations; the final group will have recalcitrant, persistent illnesses that may require lifelong care or hospitalization—though now, I suspect, the new drugs and community care models have shrunk this group considerably.

But here's the bottom line: All mental illnesses are treatable.

Often, brain chemistry has to be adjusted with medication. If symptoms occur, go to the doctor. Don't downplay it, don't hide it—seek treatment immediately. Mental illness is no more embarrassing than diabetes. And the earlier we get treatment, the more effective it will be. I myself could never have made it through this past year of grief and depression without counseling and medication. As Josh proved, very real, valid and full lives can be lived within these illnesses.

Now my husband and I sit discreetly at the very back of the *Western Union*, right behind the captain at the wheel. He has given the order; the crew has cried "fire in the hole" and shot off the cannon. We have covered our ears. We have gotten our complimentary wine, our conch chowder. We have listened to our shipmates talk about how much snow they left behind in Cleveland, how many grandchildren they have, and how one guy played hockey for Hopkins on that great team in 1965. Then we duck as, with a great whoosh of the jib, we come about. We sit quietly, holding hands, hard. Now there's a lot of wind. All around us, people are putting on their jackets.

Independent of any of this, the sky puts on its big show, gearing up for sunset. The sun speeds up as it sinks lower and lower. The water turns into a sheet of silver, like a mirror.

Like Hal, Josh was a major sunset man, always looking for that legendary green flash right after the sunset, which nobody I know has ever actually seen, though everybody claims to have known somebody who has seen it. Here where sunset is a religion, we never miss the moment. In Key West the sun grows huge and spreads out when it touches the water, so that it's no longer round at all but a glowing red beehive shape that plunges down abruptly to the thunderous applause of the revelers back at Mallory Square.

"Get ready," Hal says in my ear. "But look, there's a cloud bank, it's not going to go all the way."

I twist the top of the vial in my windbreaker pocket.

The sun glows neon red, cut off at the bottom by clouds.

A hush falls over the whole crowd on board the *Western Union.* Everybody faces west. Cameras are raised. It is happening.

"Bon voyage," Hal says. Suddenly, the sun is gone. The crowd cheers. I throw the ashes out on the water behind us; like a puff of smoke, they disappear immediately into the wake. I say, "Good-bye, baby." Nobody notices. The water turns into mother of pearl, shining pink all the way from our schooner to the horizon. The scalloped edge of the puffy clouds goes from pink to gold. The crowd goes "aah." Good-bye baby. But no green flash. The crowd stretches, they move, they mill around on deck. The light fades and stars come out.

There is a theory that mental illness conveys certain gifts. Even if this sometimes seems to be the case, as in bipolar disorder's frequent association with creativity, those gifts are not worth the pain and devastating losses the illness also brings with it. Yet sometimes there are moments. . . .

I am remembering one starry summer night back in North

Carolina, the kind of breathtakingly beautiful summer night of all our dreams, when Josh and I took a long walk around our town. He'd been staying with us for several days because he was too sick to stay in his own apartment. He'd been deteriorating for months, and his doctor had arranged his admission to UNC's Neurosciences Hospital for the next morning. Josh didn't know this yet. But he was always "compliant," as they call it. We were very lucky in this. My friend's son wouldn't take his medicine and chose to live on the street; she never knew where he was. Schizophrenia is like an umbrella diagnosis covering a whole crowd of very different illnesses; but very few people with brain disorders actually become violent, despite the stereotype.

Josh liked the hospital. It was safe, and the world he'd been in that week was not safe, not at all, a world where strangers were talking about him and people he used to know inhabited other people's bodies and tables turned into spiders and all the familiar landmarks disappeared so that he couldn't find his way anywhere. He couldn't sleep, he couldn't drive, he couldn't think.

Yet on that summer night in Hillsborough, a wonderful thing happened. We were walking through the alley between the old Confederate cemetery and our backyard when we ran into our neighbor Allan.

"Hi there, Josh," Allan said.

Instead of replying, Josh sang out a single note of music.

"A flat," he said. It hung in the hot honeysuckle air.

"Nice," Allan said, passing on.

The alley ended at Tryon Street, where we stepped onto the sidewalk. A young girl hurried past.

"C sharp," Josh said, then sang it out.

The girl looked at him before she disappeared into the Presbyterian Church.

We crossed the street and walked past the young policemen getting out of his car in front of the police station.

"Middle C," Josh said, humming.

Since it was one of Hillsborough's "Last Friday" street fairs, we ran into more and more people as we headed toward the center of town. For each one, Josh had a musical note—or a chord, for a pair or a group.

"What's up?" I finally asked.

"Well, you know I have perfect pitch," he said—I nodded, though he did not—"and everybody we see has a special musical note, and I can hear every one." He broke off to sing a high chord for a couple of young teen girls, then dropped into a lower register for a retired couple eating ice-cream cones.

"Hello," another neighbor said, smiling when Josh hummed back at him.

So it went, all over town. Even some of the buildings had notes, apparently: the old Masonic Hall, the courthouse, the corner bar. Josh was singing his heart out. And almost— almost—it was a song, the symphony of Hillsborough. We were both exhilarated. We walked and walked. By the time we got back home, he was exhausted. Finally he slept. The next day, he went into the hospital.

Josh loved James Taylor, especially his song "Fire and Rain." But we were too conservative, or chickenshit, or something, to put it on his tombstone, the same way we were "not cool enough," as Josh put it, to walk down the aisle to "Purple Rain" (his idea) while he played the piano on the day we got married in 1985.

But now I say the words to Hal as the light fades slowly on the water behind us.

> I've seen fire and I've seen rain
> I've seen sunny days that I thought would never end
> I've seen lonely times when I could not find a friend
> But I always thought that I'd see you again.

Well, I won't. I know this. But what a privilege it was to live on this earth with him, what a privilege it was to be his mother. There will be a lessening of pain, there will be consolations, I can tell. But as C. S. Lewis wrote in *A Grief Observed*: "Reality never repeats. . . . that is what we should all like. The happy past restored". . . as it can never be, and maybe never was. Who's got perfect pitch, anyway? Yet to have children—or simply to experience great love for any person at all—is to throw yourself wide open to the possibility of pain at any moment. But I would not choose otherwise. Not now, not ever. Like every parent with a disabled child, my greatest fear used to be that I would die first. "I can't die," I always said whenever any risky undertaking was proposed. So now I can die. But I don't want to. Instead, I want to live as hard as I can, burning up the days in honor of his sweet, hard life.

Night falls on the schooner ride back to Key West. I clutch the bronze vial that held some of Josh's ashes, tracing its engraved design with my finger. The wind blows my hair. The young couple in front of us are making out.

"Let's get some oysters at Alonzo's," Hal says, and suddenly I realize that I'm starving.

"Look," the captain says, pointing up. "Venus."

Sure enough. Then we see the Big Dipper, Orion, Mars. Where's that French artist with the red beret? No sign of him, and no green flash, either—but stars. A whole sky full of them by the time we slide into the dock at the end of William Street.

Blue Heaven

MAY 1965

We leave Hollins at 10 a.m., six of us girls crammed into the car, Mary Withers driving. "My Girl" is on the radio. Some of us know the dates we'll meet in Chapel Hill; some don't. I don't. He is an SAE frat brother, but I can't remember his name. I am already tired. I have been up for hours, ironing my clothes, ironing my hair. At Martinsville, we stop for gas and road beer. We sing along with the radio. Now it's "Help Me, Rhonda," by the Beach Boys. We are getting hot in the car because it doesn't have any air-conditioning, but we can't open the windows much because we would mess up our hair. I keep trying to remember my date's name. We stop in Danville for more road beer. "Ticket to Ride" is on the radio. In Chapel Hill, we pull up in front of the fraternity house; all these boys stand up and walk out to the car. Oh no. What is his name? Oh no.

Later that night, much later, we walk right up the middle of Franklin Street in formal clothes, giggling and singing. Doug Clark and the Hot Nuts played at the party. My date passed out, but now I have another date. He is from Scotland Neck, which I find hysterically funny. The sun is coming up. I'm carrying my shoes. It was some party.

JUNE 1966

Summer School. I sit on the grass near the Davie Poplar, books thrown down beside me. A soft wind blows my hair. I stretch out my legs. The boy puts his head on my lap. He wears a pastel knit shirt, pastel slacks, loafers. He looks like an Easter egg. But he is a golfer. I sigh languidly. I am in love.

AUGUST 1966

It is a hot, smoky café, the smoke barely stirred by the sluggish overhead fan. The backs of my legs stick to the sticky wooden booth. This conversation is the most intense conversation I have ever had, and also the most beer I have ever drunk. It is very, very late. This is a great conversation, I can't believe how significant it is. He leans across the table toward me. He pounds on the table to make a point. With his other hand, he touches my knee under the table. He is a member of the Student Democratic Society. We light more cigarettes. I am in love.

AUGUST 1967

It is raining, and we have been walking for hours, in a light, fine drizzle that jewels the edges of everything. We are soaked through. We stop to sit on one of the gray stone walls that are everywhere in Chapel Hill. We kiss. I run my finger along the jeweled stone. This time I am really in love. Later, much later, this guy will move to Chicago, taking my life-size painting of the Supremes and breaking my heart. Eventually I will recover. He was from Connecticut and talked funny.

JUNE 1973

Finally, I move to Chapel Hill with my husband, James Seay, a poet who has gotten a job teaching at UNC. I have always wanted to live here. So has everybody else who ever went to school here, and once school is over, many of them can't stand to leave. So everybody who comes to work on our house has a Ph.D. in something: the plumber's degree is in philosophy; the painter is a historian. I am embarrassed to have all these educated people doing manual labor on my house. I offer them coffee and cake. The carpenter listens to opera while he builds bookshelves. I have second thoughts—are we cool enough to live in Chapel Hill? I won't let the children play with toy guns while the workmen are here, so they won't think we are rednecks.

SEPTEMBER 1973

It is the first day of my new job teaching language arts at Carolina Friends School. I got this job by telephone from Nashville, where I'd been teaching seventh grade at Harpeth Hall, a prestigious girls' school. There the girls wore green and gold uniforms, the school colors, and the faculty dressed up. So I'm all ready for my first day at Carolina Friends, wearing a red linen suit with a straight skirt, pearls, patent leather heels, and stockings.

Only, I can't find the school. I drive out into the countryside as directed, on narrow roads past fields and cows and split rail fences, and then finally turn onto an unpaved road that disappears ahead of me into the forest. This can't be right! Gradually I perceive a number of ramshackle buildings here and there in the trees, then a large log house, apparently built by hand, up the hill, with a sizable deck running all around it. Built by hand? Where's the school? Harpeth Hall had a stone wall around its landscaped grounds, with paved walkways running everywhere.

Finally I spot an old man in a baseball cap and overalls, trudging up the road carrying a toolbox. I pull beside him and announce, "I'm looking for Carolina Friends School."

"Well, you've found us." He gives me a big smile and sticks his hand in the window for me to shake. I had him pegged as a janitor, but maybe not.

"But where are the students?" I still haven't seen one.

He points up the hill at the log house.

"They're settling in," he says.

I stare at him.

"We start every day with meditation," he says. "Quiet time."

Really? I'm still thinking as I park in a cluster of old pickups and vans with peace signs on them. I have never known any middle school students to be capable of quiet time, much less meditation. It's pretty hard walking up the pebbly dirt road in these patent leather heels, covered by dust when I finally make it.

Nobody seems to be around, so I go on in the open door, mortified to find myself suddenly in the midst of about seventy people, young and old, all of them down on the polished wood floor, where they form a huge, ragged circle in every posture imaginable, heads mostly bowed, eyes mostly closed. Everybody's wearing blue jeans, cut-offs, or shorts, with sneakers, flip-flops—or simply bare feet. There's a giant, colorful hand-woven mandala on the wall above them. Across the big room I spot a guy I somehow know to be Don Wells, the head of the school, the guy who hired me on the phone. He's got long, blondish hair, he's sitting crosslegged, grinning at me. He does not get up. Out of some wrong-headed perversity I pick my way through the meditating students, across the open part of the circle, my heels clicking on the wood floor. Nobody says a word. But when I have almost made it, here comes a long, single, expert wolf whistle, and then a rising chorus of other wolf whistles. Oh no. I feel myself turning as red as this smart little red suit, which I will never, ever, wear again. The guy Don gets up and hugs me, laughing. Now everybody is laughing, scrambling to their feet, heading outdoors. Another teacher brings me some sandals so I can participate in the ropes course and the relay races and the trust-building exercises. Well, some of them, anyway.

I'm getting the drill—or the lack of the drill, I should say. They have no uniforms and no school colors and no sports except for Ultimate Frisbee, whatever that is. I stand out on the deck looking down at the hilly, wooded landscape covered with kids and grownups in all kinds of activities that are, I realize suddenly, much less random than they seem. This will turn out to be true of everything.

I am surprised and horrified to hear my first assignment, which is to plan and buy the food for a hundred people for one day of our upcoming weekend retreat at Quaker Lake.

"I don't know anything about feeding that many people. I just can't do that," I tell Don.

"Oh, sure you can," Don says.

At my first faculty meeting that afternoon, I have to settle in, too. Then Don welcomes me and asks, "What individual courses do you want to teach?"

"Well, what are the requirements?" I ask. "I mean, the curriculum."

"We're in the process of figuring that out," Don says. "You tell me."

Everybody speaks up. They all listen to each other. They all have great ideas. I have no ideas. In fact, I'm having a panic attack, but then after a while something else starts happening. Somewhere, way down inside, it's like a dam gives way and I start getting excited. I love plays, I have always wanted kids to write plays and then put them on. I have always wanted to teach a class that mixes up art and writing, or photography and writing, I have always wanted to teach ghost stories, and Greek mythology, and poetry out loud, really loud. Also I've got this recipe for taco pie casserole that might work great for that retreat.

SUMMER, MID-1970S

A party on Stinson Street, probably Anne Jones's house. Everybody I know has lived on Stinson Street at one time or another. Stinson Street has constant parties, constant yard sales. Anyway, at some point during one of these parties, I go outside to get some air and wander across the street to Leonard Rogoff's yard sale, where I stand transfixed before a chest of drawers with a mirror attached to the top of it. I stand before the chest and look into the mirror for a long time. The mirror is tilted so that I can see a tree, the moon, my face. Oh no, I think. This is really my life, and I am really living it. I remember thinking that then, on Stinson Street.

LATE 1970S, EARLY 1980S

I sit on the edge of the Rainbow Soccer Field, where my kids are playing Rainbow Soccer, which is noncompetitive. You can't yell anything like "Kill 'em!" or "Stomp 'em!" This is hard for some parents. My son Josh is playing center forward. I am writing a novel.

I sit at the Chapel Hill Tennis Club, waiting for my son's match to start. This is my son Page. He's real good. I am writing a novel.

I sit on a wing chair before the fire in the Chapel Hill Public Library on Franklin Street . . . in a booth at Breadmen's . . . at a picnic table at University Lake . . . on a quilt at Umstead Park . . . in a wicker chair on my own back porch on Burlage Circle. I am writing a novel. I am always writing a novel in this town. Nobody cares. Nobody bugs me. Nobody thinks a thing about it. Everybody else is writing a novel, too.

"In Chapel Hill, throw a rock and you'll hit a writer," someone once said. This has always been true. For Chapel Hill is primarily a town of the mind, a town of trees and visions. Thomas Wolfe praised the "rare romantic quality of the atmosphere." Maybe the quiet, leafy streets themselves are still informed by his giant spirit, that wild young man from the mountains who raged through them in his archetypal search for identity.

The much-loved UNC English professor Hugh Holman wrote, "The primary thing that Chapel Hill gives those who come to be a part of it is the freedom to be themselves. It is an unorganized town. It is easy to persuade its citizens, along with the students of the university, to join briefly in a cause, to march for a little while beneath a banner . . . but to remain permanently organized is something else indeed, for Chapel Hill does not organize very well. Those who come to this town can find in it just about the quantity of freedom to be themselves which they wish to have."

CIRCA 1980

I am with my children, and we run into some of their friends from their former community church preschool, along with the friends' mother.

"Hello, Naomi," I say. "Hi, Johnny."

"We have changed our names," their mother says. "This is Trumpet Vine," she indicates Naomi, "and this is Golden Sun. I myself am Flamingo."

Oh my, I think. Oh no. My kids do not think that Trumpet Vine is a very good name. But then my younger son, Page, changes his own name (briefly) to Rick. He has always hated Page, a family name; he gets teased because it is too girly. Soon after this, Trumpet Vine, Golden Sun, and Flamingo moved away from Chapel Hill with some kind of sect, I think they were called the Orange People.

I never changed my name, but I have thought about it ever since. I would go with three syllables, too: Biloxi, Chardonnay, Sunflower . . .

SURPRISES, SPRING 1981

In retrospect, it seems inevitable. Both people of good will, my husband and I have been kept together by children and family and friends and common interests, but we are very different. When he suddenly moves out, I am traumatized. I am thirty-seven, old as the hills, old as dirt. And now I am getting a divorce. My mother bursts into tears. "Nobody in our family has *evah* gotten a divorce," she weeps, though later she will admit that a numbah of them should have. My mountain father weighs in with his mountain advice: "Change the locks and get a handgun." I don't do that. I do lose twenty pounds, almost overnight. In fact I lose everything, leaving jackets and purses all over town. I let my boys ride their skateboards through our empty house and eat exclusively from the Red Food Group so beloved by boys (SpaghettiOs, Hawaiian Punch, bacon, barbecued potato chips). I take them skiing in Colorado with my cousins for spring break.

I desperately need a real job instead of the part-time position I've got. Suddenly one comes up at North Carolina State University, full-time. Only I don't have the nerve to apply for it, I don't have the academic credentials. "Don't give me that crap," my friend and fellow writer Doris Betts says. "Just go for it." She pushes me into it, and to my surprise I get the job, which I will keep for nineteen years.

On Valentine's Day I get myself together, as my mother used to say, and go out for an afternoon Valentine party thrown by

Marilyn Hartman, who directs the Evening College at Duke University, where I teach creative writing once a week. Here I meet another writer, a journalist named Hal Crowther, a recent transplant from Buffalo who is teaching critical writing in this same program. I know who he is, I have been admiring his columns in the new *Spectator* magazine. We start talking and it turns out that we have both stashed our children in video parlors so we can come to this party. Then we start talking about Robert Stone's recent novel, *A Flag for Sunrise*, which we have both just read. Hal keeps rattling his tiny cup in his tiny saucer and looking for wine. But there's only tea. "Would you like to go out for a drink sometime?" he asks.

A man is the last thing I'm looking for, but I'm not a fool, either. "Sure," I hear myself saying from a great distance as I levitate over the Valentine party, something I have been doing a lot lately.

Soon after that I have to go to a meeting at N.C. State, so I meet Hal for lunch at a restaurant in Raleigh. But I am so nervous, I lean forward right in the middle of this lunch and say, "Well, how do you think this is going? Because I'm so nervous I would just as soon bag it if we're not having fun." Hal says he is having fun, so I keep on seeing him.

"Cut it out," my friends say. "This is supposed to be your interim man."

I write a country song named "Interim Man." I keep on seeing Hal.

Hal's daughter, Amity, is ten and very beautiful, all legs and big blue eyes, very feminine and very sophisticated. An only child, she has spent lots of time with adults, especially her adoring father. This is the first entire summer day she has spent alone at my house, while my boys are at a tennis day camp and her father is in Raleigh at work.

"Well, Amity, what would you like for lunch?" I ask her. "Would you rather have a grilled cheese sandwich or a peanut butter and jelly sandwich?"

She hesitates. "How about French bread and brie?" she says, used to little gourmet picnics with her dad.

All I have is Velveeta and Wonder.

But we bridge the yawning culture gap between us as the summer goes on. For one thing, Amity actually likes to go to the grocery store with me, a thing my boys can't stand. And we both like to cook, especially cakes. We bake cake after cake for the ravenous boys while my visiting mother, a former home economics teacher, calls out measurements from her reclining position on the sofa.

All three of us—me, my mother, and Amity—read the *National Enquirer* and *The Midnight Sun* from cover to cover as soon as we get them home from the grocery store. We especially love UFO abductions and multiple births and anything at all about Elvis. (This *National Enquirer* habit is Amity's own mother's only complaint about my parenting skills . . . though, Lord

knows, she has plenty of other things to choose from as well.)
But I claim that I am doing research for a novel named *Lives of
the Stars*, which turns out to be sort of true anyway.

One day Hal and I are reading the newspaper and I read that
genius woman's column and say, "Guess what? There is no other
word in the English language that rhymes with 'orange.'"

Hal thinks for a minute. "What about Warren G. Harding?"
he says.

Okay. I am in love.

SPRING 1982

Hal and I are walking in the woods, following one of the green-
space trails that run all over town, when suddenly we come
upon a life-size concrete hippo, climbing out of Bolin Creek
as if emerging from the Blue Nile. Oh no, I think stupidly, a
hippo! Anything can happen in Chapel Hill. I realize that we'll
probably get married.

JANUARY 1983

A Snapshot of the End of My Youth. Chapel Hill Community
Center. A recreation-department basketball game is in progress.
My son's team, the Tigers, is ahead by two points, but it's nip
and tuck all the way. "Shoot, Monty, shoot!" yells somebody's
father, sitting next to me. For some reason, I turn around and
look at this father. He's an attractive black man wearing a leather
hat and a diamond ring. For some reason, he looks familiar.

Then it hits me. Oh no! It's Doug Clark! of Doug Clark and the Hot Nuts! He's got a kid, Monty, on the opposing team . . . oh no. I am really old.

SUMMER 1983. THE BEEHIVE

I drive from my house on Burlage Circle over toward the university on Franklin Street along those old stone walls on a hot, green summer day, which reminds me of that first time I ever came to Chapel Hill for summer school so long ago. Now I am going to visit Dr. Louis Rubin, who has retired from teaching English (and Southern Literature, which he invented) in order to start a publishing company, of all things. It is located in the garage behind his old stone house on Gimghoul Road. A sign on the fence reads: ALGONQUIN BOOKS OF CHAPEL HILL, EDITORIAL OFFICES. PLEASE KEEP GATE CLOSED AGAINST DOG.

Louis Rubin was my creative writing teacher at Hollins for four years, which is why I still call him Mr. Rubin. I couldn't call him Louis if my life depended upon it. Mr. Rubin was a great, great teacher who changed my life, as he has changed so many others. In fact it is probable that I would never have become a writer at all if I had not encountered him when I did, because I was a wild girl, and I'm not sure what would have happened to me. But I do know for sure that if I am ever able to write anything real, or beautiful, or honest—anything that ever speaks truly about the human condition—it will be due to this man.

I enter carefully through the gate and go into the garage.

It's like a beehive in here. I say hello to Mimi Fountain, also from Hollins, Ann Moss, and Garrett Epps. Shannon Ravenel, Mr. Rubin's partner in this enterprise, works from St. Louis. Mr. Rubin has just written her a letter about their new venture: "This is going to be fun, I think." In the newspaper he has said, "Editing is just like teaching, but publishing is something else. I don't want to just put new people into print; I want to launch them." Right now Mr. Rubin is making a peanut butter sandwich on top of an old filing cabinet in the back, where he will eat it, standing up. He does this every day. All around him, manuscripts rise to his knees.

The FedEx man comes in and the dog runs out, then we all run out after the dog. The postman comes. Eva Rubin drives back from her job teaching political science at N.C. State. She waves and goes into the house, followed by the miscreant dog. Now Mr. Rubin feeds the birds, which means throwing several handfuls of seed straight up into the air. The sky goes black with birds and beating wings. I start squealing and batting at them. Mr. Rubin is laughing. Finally the birds fly away and he looks at me. "Whatcha got?" he asks and I hand him the pages I've brought, all wrinkled up and sweaty from me holding them.

I follow him inside the house to his office where he sticks a cigar in his mouth and sits down and starts reading immediately. Mr. Rubin never does anything later. "I know it's got too many voices in it," I say when he gets done, but he grins and hands it back.

"Keep on going," he says, which is all he needs to say and all I need to hear, because I am already thinking what comes next, and I can't even remember driving home.

JUNE 29, 1985

Amity, age thirteen and very grown up, has specified a church wedding for her father and me, and so here we are at the Chapel of the Cross, rehearsing hurriedly for our tiny 10 a.m. ceremony, which will take place in less than an hour. Radiant in her white dress, Amity walks endlessly up and down the aisle carrying her bouquet, carrying herself just so. She looks beautiful. But the ladies arranging the flowers at the altar scowl at her, whispering among themselves, casting dark looks at the middle-aged groom.

Finally one of the ladies says acidly to me, "Just how old is she, anyway?" and I realize that they think she's the bride, not me in my green linen dress. Oh no. This is what I get for fancying myself a bride at my age! I ought to know better. I ought to stay single and write novels out in the woods.

But then, forty minutes later, I am the bride, and I am the happiest bride ever, as the organ plays and the bells ring and we step out into the bright June day married, of all things, and my boys wave at some other boys who are skating on skateboards down Franklin Street.

THANKSGIVING 1985, '86, '87, '88 . . .

For many years we hold the Wild Turkey Classic every Thanksgiving. Originally it was Hal's idea to go out and play a couple innings of softball before the big traditional dinner in the afternoon. I jumped right on it. Genius! A morning softball game gives the kids and the visiting relatives and friends something to do (and keeps us all from drinking too much) during those long hours while the turkey roasts and those floats roll interminably down Fifth Avenue on TV. The baseball diamond at Phillips Junior High is right up the street. Hal makes some calls, especially to other diehard Durham Bulls fans like himself. I tell friends and neighbors. I make the dressing and mash the potatoes ahead of time.

Thanksgiving Day dawns clear and cold with a brilliant Carolina blue sky. Hal heads for the field early, taking bats and bases and gloves and his brother Jeff, who is reputed to have been scouted by the Yankees but right now is hung over. Hal pushes him out the door, not easy. I've already got the turkey in the oven, covered with tons of butter and several old kitchen towels and tin foil—my substitute for basting. I corral the wild boys and fill up the station wagon with dogs, kids, juice, store-bought doughnuts and coffeecake and a folding table to put it all out on. We turn right off Estes and head up to the raised grassy baseball field, which looms like some kind of Indian mound or ancient fort. Coming up over the hill I stop amazed at the scene before me, like a Brueghel painting. Who are all these people? I guess the word spread. People are everywhere, doing knee bends, running, tossing the ball back and forth, talking, hugging, hugging. Lots of hugging. I set up my table and talk intensely with friends I haven't seen for years. People spread quilts on the sidelines. Somebody has brought a brand new baby in a little yellow suit, and he is passed around and admired. Laughter rings out like bells. Our breath makes white puffs in the chilly blue air, cartoon conversation. Kids and dogs cover the outfield. Now whistles are blowing. They're already choosing sides. It's Michael McFee vs. Jay Bryan . . . two poets! Whoever thought the poets would be competitive? But they're cool, choosing wimpy kids like my own as well as grownups. Each side has got about thirty players. Bill Leuchtenburg, in his seventies, is playing second. Jimmy Mills, very slightly younger, is at third. A huge scream goes up when a yellow lab snatches the ball and runs off into the trees with it.

"PLAY BALL!" somebody hollers, and then we do, for the next twenty years or so, as the Massengale boys and the Ludingtons grow up before our very eyes and other kids go away and get married and then come back with their own kids, first in strollers and then on the field, another generation. Some people divorce and return with other people. Some people go to graduate school in Iowa, or to rehab, or New York or Asheville or Austin, places too far to come back from. Every year, more girls are playing, not only our perennial Elva, a ringer.

Bill Leuchtenburg is still playing second. Jim Watson still bikes to the game wearing that Duke hat, his hair flying out behind him. All of Amity's boyfriends have to come and play ball, this is a requirement. On and on it goes, year after year, on sunny Thursdays and cloudy Thursdays and freezing Thursdays, in fog, in sleet, the sweet taste of doughnuts, the crack of the bat, the screams and yells and laughter of the crowd, old friends and new, all these dear and changing faces, these lovers of the game.

JUNE 2012

Hal and I have lived in Hillsborough for sixteen years now, so it's not often I find myself driving alone through Chapel Hill this late at night, windows down, after a concert with friends. I glimpse a little sliver of moon above the moving treetops. Maybe because it's that precious time at the end of the semester, before summer school has started, but it's quiet as quiet can be tonight on Franklin Street, no people and no other cars, only a little breeze rustling the thick leaves on all these big trees and bringing me the unbearably sweet and somehow sad scent of honeysuckle. This reminds me of eating dinner one June night at Crook's Corner when Bill Smith had just invented his famous honeysuckle sorbet, which he brought out to our table, and it was true, I could taste it, all the inexpressible longing of honeysuckle as it melted on my tongue. Now the breeze brings laughter, and music from far away. All those years, all that music . . . starting with Bland Simpson and Jim Wann's early seventies performance of *Diamond Studs* at the old Ranch House restaurant on Airport Road, everybody dancing on the tables to "Cakewalk in Kansas City, " I had never seen anything like it, "musicians' theater" they called it, and they would take it straight to Broadway. . . . And always, Jim Watson's annual Christmas show at the Cave . . . and Callie Warner singing the title song of our own show *Good Ol' Girls* in its first production at Swain Hall right here on campus. I remember Tommy Thompson of the Red Clay Ramblers singing his "Hot Buttered Rum," one of the most beautiful songs in the world, at the old Cat's Cradle in the dead of winter. Most of all I remember my son Josh sitting down at the piano in our Akai Hana sushi restaurant to play his own signature jazz set, "Five Not So Easy Pieces" he used to call it, which always included "Pachelbel," those running purely joyous notes, a celebration. The music of this night comes closer now, and the laughter, and then I see them, barefooted girls four abreast walking down the middle of the street, long hair swinging, singing. That blonde, second from the left, looks somehow familiar to me as she doubles over in laughter and almost falls, oh she's got no idea what's going to happen to her in the years to come, she doesn't care, either. All she wants is now, and she wants it bad, and I want her to have it all. But then the van ahead of me stops to let some people out and when I can see again, they're gone, those girls, she's gone, my girl, if she ever was there at all.

A Life in Books

I WAS A READER LONG BEFORE I was a writer. In fact, I started writing in the first place because I couldn't stand for my favorite books to be over, so I started adding more and more chapters onto the ends of them, often including myself as a character. Thus the Bobbsey twins became the Bobbsey triplets, and Nancy Drew's best friends, Bess Marvin and George Fayne, were joined by another character named Lee Smith—who actually ended up with Ned Nickerson! The additional chapters grew longer and more complicated as my favorite books became more complicated—*Heidi*, *Anne of Green Gables*, and *Pippi Longstocking*, for instance.

Mama was indefatigable in reading aloud to me when I was little, and I'm sure that the musical cadence of her soft Southern voice is one reason I took to reading the way I did, for the activity itself was so pleasurable. Later, we pored over the huge pages of the *National Enquirer* together, marveling at the lives of the stars, the psychic who could bend spoons with the power of his mind alone, and that Indiana couple who got kidnapped and taken away in a space ship where they were given physical examinations by aliens before being dropped back down into their own cornfield, none the worse for wear. Mama and I loved this stuff. My father read a lot of newspapers, magazines, and sometimes history or politics. Though neither of my parents read novels, they received the *Reader's Digest* Condensed Books, which I devoured, and they also encouraged me to go to our fledgling library.

This soon got out of hand. I became a voracious, then an obsessive reader; recurrent bouts of pneumonia and tonsillitis gave me plenty of time to indulge my passion. After I was pronounced "sickly," I got to stay home a lot, slathered with a vile salve named Mentholatum, spirit lamp hissing in the corner of my room, reading to my heart's content. I remained an inveterate reader of the sort who hides underneath the covers with a flashlight and reads all night long. But I did not read casually, or for mere information. What I wanted was to feel all wild and trembly inside, an effect first produced by *The Secret Garden*, which I'd read maybe twenty times.

The only man I had ever loved as much as Colin of *The Secret Garden* was Johnny Tremain, from Esther Forbes' book of that title. I used to wish it was *me*—not Johnny Tremain—who'd had the hot silver spilled on my hand. I would have suffered anything (everything!) for Johnny Tremain.

Other books had affected me strongly: *Little Women,* especially the part where Beth dies, and *Gone With the Wind,* especially the part where Melanie dies. I had long hoped for a wasting disease, such as leukemia, to test my mettle. I also loved *Marjorie Morningstar, A Tree Grows in Brooklyn,* and books like *Dear and Glorious Physician, The Shoes of the Fisherman, Christy,* and anything at all about horses and saints. I had read all the Black Stallion books, of course, as well as all the Marguerite Henry books. But my all-time favorite was a book about Joan of Arc, especially the frontispiece illustration depicting Joan as she knelt and "prayed without ceasing for guidance from God," whose face was depicted overhead in a thunderstorm. Not only did I love Joan of Arc, I wanted to *be* her.

I was crazy for horses and saints.

"By the way," my mother mentioned to me one day almost casually while I was home being sick in bed and she was straightening my covers, "You know, Marguerite Henry stayed at your grandmother's boarding house on Chincoteague Island while she was writing that book."

"What book?" I sat right up.

"*Misty,*" Mama said. "Then she came back to write *Sea Star,* and I think the illustrator, Wesley Dennis, stayed there, too. Cousin Jack used to take him out on a boat."

I couldn't believe it! A real writer, a horse writer, had walked up the crushed oyster shell road where I had gone barefoot, had sat at the big dinner table where I'd eaten fish and corncakes for breakfast; had maybe even swung in the same wicker porch swing I loved.

I wrote a novel on the spot, on eight sheets of my mother's Crane stationery. It featured as main characters my two favorite people at that time: Adlai Stevenson and Jane Russell. In my novel, they fell in love and then went West together in a covered wagon. Once there they got married and became— inexplicably!—Mormons. I am not sure how I knew about Mormons. But even at that age, I was fixed upon romance, flight, and religion, themes I would return to again and again.

What did my parents think of this strange little girl who had come to them so late in life, after they had become resigned to never having children? Well, they spoiled me rotten and were simply delighted by everything I did, everything I showed any interest in. I believe if I had told my mother that I wanted to be, say, an ax murderer, she would have said, without blinking an eye, "Well, that's nice, dear, what do you think you might want to major in?" My daddy would have gone out to buy me the ax.

Though my parents might feel—as Mama certainly said, later—that they wished I would just stop all that writing stuff and marry a lawyer or a doctor, which is what a daughter really ought to do, of course, the fact is that they were so loving that they gave me the confidence, and the permission, early on, to do just about anything I wanted to do. Decades later, I would realize how unusual this was, and how privileged I have been because of it. Now I see this issue—permission to write—as the key issue for many women I have worked with in my classes, especially women who have begun writing later in their lives.

But my childhood was not entirely a happy one. No writer's childhood ever is. There was my father's inexplicable sadness and my mother's "nerves"; there was my strange Uncle Tick; there was a scary little neighborhood "club" we formed, which did bad things. There was a lot of drinking. There were hospitalizations and long absences and periods of being sent away to live with other relatives. Life was often confusing and mysterious, which inspired Martha Sue and my cousin Randy and me to start our own espionage firm, which I would describe much later in a short story named "Tongues of Fire":

We lived to spy, and this is mainly what we did on our bike trips around town. We'd seen some really neat stuff, too. For instance we had seen Roger Ainsley, the coolest guy in our school, squeezing pimples in his bathroom mirror. We had seen Mister Bondurant whip his son Earl with a belt, and later, when Earl suddenly dropped out of school and enlisted in the Army, we alone knew why. We had seen our fourth-grade teacher, prissy Miss Emily Horn, necking on a couch with her boyfriend, and smoking cigarettes. Best of all, we had seen Mrs. Cecil Hertz come running past a picture window wearing nothing but an apron, followed shortly by Mr. Cecil Hertz himself, wearing nothing at all and carrying a spatula.

It was amazing how careless people were about drawing their drapes and pulling their shades down. It was amazing what you could see, especially if you were an athletic and enterprising girl such as myself. I wrote my observations down in a Davy Crockett spiral notebook I'd bought for this purpose. I wrote down everything: date, time, weather, physical descriptions, my reaction. I would use all this stuff later, in my novels.

This is true. And though it's also true that we actually did spy on people, that first paragraph is mostly made up. When you write fiction, you up the ante, generally speaking, since real life rarely affords enough excitement or conflict to spice up a page sufficiently. This passage also illustrates another technique that has saved my neck—maybe even my life—many times: the use of humor to allow us to talk or write about the scariest things, things we couldn't articulate and deal with otherwise. It is another way of whistling past the graveyard.

MY FIRST ACTUAL NOVEL WAS named *The Last Day the Dogbushes Bloomed* (1969), and its main character was a weird little nine-year-old girl named Susan, much like this very same nine-year-old girl we have been talking about. She was often a solitary child, though her imaginary friends and pursuits were legion. In this excerpt, she describes a favorite hideout, her "wading house."

The way to the wading house was hard. That's what was so good about it. After I got there, no scouts could track me down. First I went out from under the other side of the dogbushes, then I went by a secret path through the blackberry bushes, which tried to grab me as I went by. They reached out their hands at me but I got away. When I came to the riverbank, I walked on the rocks to the wading house. That way, if anybody chased me with dogs, they would lose the trail.

The wading house was not a real house. It was a soft, light green tree, a willow that grew by the bank. The way the branches came down, they made a little house inside them. The land and the tiny river were both inside the house, and it was the only wading house in the world, and I was the only one that knew about it. It was a very special place. There were a lot of other people that lived there too and they were my good friends. There was a young lizard named Jerry, because I didn't know if it was a boy or a girl, and Jerrys can go either way. Jerry had a long, shiny tail and he stayed mostly in the weeds but he would come out to say hello to me every time I came. A very wise old grandfather turtle lived there too. He blinked his eyes slow at me, and I could tell that he knew everything there was to know. Grandfather Turtle had three silly daughters, but I liked them because they were so cute. Their shells were like the rug in the Trivettes' living room, brown and green by turns. The big rock by the side of the river was not a rock at all, it was a secret apartment house. A baby blacksnake sat on the top. He was so black and fast that it hurt you to look at him. On the second floor, the sides of the rock, there lived a family of little brown bugs. They were always busy and never had much time to play. The worms did, though. They lived on the ground floor under the rock, and I liked them almost best of all. I never knew a family that had so much fun. All they ever did was wiggle and laugh.

After I said hi to everybody in the wading house I liked to sit under the big tree on the bank and think about a lot of things. There were a lot of things to think about then, and there was nothing to keep from thinking about like there is now. Or sometimes I would sit, like that day, and look at everything very hard so it would stay in my head for always.

What this little narrator is trying very hard not to think about is that her family is breaking up because the mother has run off with a man. This was an entirely fictional plot, of course, but a novel must have conflict; conflict is the single absolutely necessary ingredient of fiction.

As soon as my book was accepted, I was really excited, of course, and sent a copy to my parents. I waited anxiously for their reply, but I heard nothing. Nothing. Finally I called them up on the "long-distance telephone," as we used to say then.

My mother answered.

"Have you read my book?" I asked.

"Yes, I have," she said.

"Well, how did you like it?" I asked.

"Not much," my mother said. "In fact, I have thrown it in the river."

"*What?*" I said. "What's wrong with it?"

"Everybody in this town is going to think I ran off with a man," my mother said.

"Mama, that's just crazy," I said. "Look, you're still there. You and Daddy have been married for thirty years."

"It doesn't matter," my mother said. "That's what they'll think anyway. So I am taking steps to make sure that they are not going to read it, any of them."

"Wait a minute," I said. "What steps?"

"I have told your father that he cannot order the book," she said—my father's Ben Franklin dimestore being naturally the only place in town where you could possibly buy a book—"And I have told Lillian Elgin that she cannot order the book either." Mama's friend, Lillian Elgin, was the town librarian.

So, that was it! Total censorship! Nobody in town ever read that first book, or the second book either. My mother banned that one because it had sex in it. But that was just as well, I guess, because it was also just awful, as second novels sometimes are if we write them too soon, having used up our entire life so far, all the great traumas and dramas of our youth, in the first one. My second was all about a sensitive English major who keeps having disastrous yet generic romances; luckily, publishing it was exactly like throwing it in the river.

BUT NOW I WAS IN big trouble, as a writer. I had used up my childhood, I had used up my adolescence, and I had nothing more to say. I had used up my whole life! Furthermore I was happily married to the poet James Seay, my first husband, so there was also no conflict, that necessary cauldron of creativity.

But luckily, by then I was a reporter working at *The Tuscaloosa News* in Tuscaloosa, Alabama, where my editor assigned me to cover the all-south majorette contest taking place on the campus of the University of Alabama. This was an enormous contest with categories you might expect—such as "Fire Baton" and "Best Personality"—but also a lot of categories you might not expect, such as "Improvisation to a Previously Unheard Tune," which I thought was a riot. The winner of the whole thing would be called Miss Fancy Strut. The girls were really sweet, because they were all trying to get Miss Personality, which would give them a lot of extra points, but their mothers were just bitches from hell, very competitive. Anyway, it lasted for days, and then finally all the points from all the categories were tallied up, and the winner turned out to be a beautiful little blonde girl from Opp, Alabama, whom I had to interview.

So I asked, of course, "How does it feel to be Miss Fancy Strut?"

And she said, with tears streaming down her face, "This is the happiest moment of my life!"

I was completely stunned, because I could tell this was true, and I was thinking, Oh honey, it's going to be a long downhill slide from here. You are so young to peak out like this.

You will not be surprised to learn that my next novel was named *Fancy Strut*, and it was all about majorettes and their mamas. It was a real breakthrough for me, because nobody in it was anything like me at all. Finally I had made that necessary imaginative leap—which is a real necessity, since most of us writers can't be out there living like crazy all the time. These days, very few are the writers whose book jackets list things like bush pilot, big game hunter, or exotic dancer.

No, more often we are English teachers. We have children, we have mortgages, we have bills to pay. So we have to stop writing strictly about what we know, which is what they always told us to do in creative writing classes. Instead, we have to write about what we can learn, and what we can imagine, and thus we come to experience that great pleasure Anne Tyler noted when somebody asked her why she writes, and she answered, "I write because I want more than one life." Let me repeat that: "I write because I want more than one life."

And let me tell you, this is the greatest privilege, and the greatest pleasure, in the world. Over the years I have moved away from autobiography to write about housewives and whores, serpent handlers and beauticians, country music singers and evangelists and nineteenth-century schoolteachers—lots of people I will never be, living in times and places I have never been. But somewhere along the way, I have also come to realize that the correspondences between real life and fiction are infinitely more complicated than I would have ever guessed as a younger woman.

Peter Taylor once said, "I write in order to find out what I think." This is certainly true for me, too, and often I don't even know what I think until I go back and read what I've written. My belief is that we have only one life, that this is all there is. And I refuse to lead an unexamined life. No matter how painful it may be, I want to know what's going on. So I write fiction the way other people write in their journals.

My husband, Hal, has been heard to bemoan my lack of self-knowledge. He envisions our respective psyches like this: his is a big room in a factory, brightly lit. He's got uniformed guys in there carrying clipboards and constantly working on all his problems, checking gauges and levels, in day and night shifts. He's always monitoring their work, reading their reports. He sees my mind, by contrast, as a dark forest with no path, where huge beasts loom up at you suddenly out of the night and then disappear, only to return again and again.

Maybe so. But when I read what I've written, I know what they are.

In 1980, for instance, I wrote a novel named *Black Mountain Breakdown*, about a girl named Crystal Spangler who is so busy fitting herself into others' images of her (first fulfilling her mother's beauty-queen dreams, then altering her image to please the various men in her life) that she loses her own true self and finally ends up paralyzed: "Crystal just lies up there in that room every day, with her bed turned catty-corner so she could look out the window and see Lorene's climbing rambler rose in full bloom on the trellis if she would turn her head. But she won't. She won't lift a finger. She just lies there. Everybody in town takes a fancy to it" . . . feeding her jello, brushing her hair, reading *The Reader's Digest* out loud to her. The most terrifying aspect of her condition is that "Crystal is happy . . . as outside her window the seasons come and go and the colors change on the mountain." When I wrote that, my first marriage should have ended years earlier, something I'd been unable to face or even admit; later, reading those words over, I finally understood how I'd felt during the last part of that marriage. I was able then to deal with its inevitable ending, and move on with my life.

No matter what I may think I am writing about at any given time—majorettes in Alabama, or a gruesome, long-ago murder, or the history of country music—I have come to realize that it is all, finally, about me, often in some complicated way I won't come to understand until years later. But then it will be there for me to read, and I will understand it, and even if I don't know who I am now, I will surely have a record of who I was then.

WRITING IS ALSO MY ADDICTION, for the moment when I am writing fiction is that moment when I am most intensely alive. This "aliveness" does not seem to be mental, or not exactly. I am certainly not thinking while I write. Whatever I'm doing is almost the opposite of thinking. Especially during the pre-writing phase, when I am simply making up the story and imagining its characters, and during those first drafts, I feel a dangerous, exhilarating sense that anything can happen.

It reminds me of a woman in eastern Kentucky I interviewed years ago when I was writing about serpent-handling believers. I had seen her lift a double handful of copperheads high in the air during a religious service. Now we faced each other across a little Formica table in a fast-food restaurant, drinking Cokes and eating fries. I asked the obvious: "Why do you do this, when it's so dangerous? You could die any time." She merely smiled at me, a beautiful, generous smile without a trace of irony.

"Honey," she began, "I do it out of an intense desire for holiness." She smiled at me again, while that sank in. "And I'll tell you something else, too. When you've held the serpent in your hands, the whole world kind of takes on an edge for you."

I could see that. Chill bumps arose on my arms as she spoke.

For I was once the girl who had embarrassed her mother so much by rededicating my life over and over at various revivals, coming home dripping wet from total immersion in those standup pools from Sears that they set up in the little tents behind the big revival tents, or simply in the fast-flowing creeks that rushed down the mountainsides.

And the feeling I get when I'm writing intensely is much the same.

For me, writing is a physical joy. It is almost sexual—not the moment of fulfillment, but the moment when you open the door to the room where your lover is waiting, and everything else falls away.

It does fall away, too. For the time of the writing, I am nobody. Nobody at all. I am a conduit, nothing but a way for the story to come to the page. Oh, but I am terribly alive then, too, though I say I am no one at all; my every sense is keen and quivering. I can smell the bacon cooking downstairs in my grandmother's kitchen that winter morning in 1952, I can feel the flowered carpet under my bare feet as I run down the hall, I can see the bright blue squares of the kitchen wallpaper, bunches of cherries alternating with little floral bouquets. Sun shines through the frost on the windowpanes, almost blinding me; my grandaddy's Lucky Strike cigarette smoke still hangs in the air, lazy blue, though he is already up and gone, he has walked the bridge across the river to the old stone courthouse where he will work all day long as the county treasurer. I love my granddaddy, who always wears a hat and a dark blue suit. I do not love my grandmother so much, who tells me not to be a tomboy and keeps moistening her lips with her tongue in a way I hate. I wish my mother would get out of the hospital so I could go home. I don't see why I can't stay with Daddy, anyway. I could make us peanut butter sandwiches for dinner, and cut the crusts off.

See what mean? I am there now, and I want to stay there. I hate to leave that kitchen and come back to this essay.

All my senses are involved when I am writing fiction, but it is hearing that is most acute. This has always been true. I can see everything in the story, of course—I have to see that kitchen in order to walk through it; the icy river, in order to get my grandfather across the bridge. I make a lot of maps before I start writing, Scotch-taping them to the wall. But I am not a visual person in real life. I never know how high to hang pictures, for instance, or where the furniture should go. None of my clothes match. It was words I loved first, words and sentences and music and stories, the voice that comes out of the dark when you're almost asleep, sitting in somebody's lap on a porch, trying to keep your eyes open long enough to hear the end of the story.

So a story always comes to me in a human voice, speaking not exactly into my ear but somewhere deep inside me. If I am writing from a first-person point of view, it is always the voice of the person who is telling the story. If I am writing from a third-person point of view, it is simply the voice of the story itself. Sometimes this voice is slow and pondering, or tentative and unsure. Sometimes it is flat and reportorial: just the facts, ma'am. Sometimes it's gossipy, intimate—a tale told over a Coke and a cigarette during a work break at Food City. Sometimes it's sad, a long, wailing lament, telling and retelling again and again how he done me wrong. It can be furious or vengeful: "I hated him from the moment I first laid eyes on him, hated him instinctively, as if I knew somehow what he would do to our family . . ." It can be a reliable narrator—or an unreliable narrator, sometimes even more interesting. It can be a meditative, authoritative voice, told as if from the distant past or from a great and somehow definitive distance (I confess that ever since we moved into this old house where I work in an upstairs office looking out over the town, this has happened more frequently!)

The most thrilling, of course, is when it is a first-person voice telling a story of real urgency. At these times, all I have to do is keep up; I become a stenographer, a court secretary, a tape recorder. My biggest job is making sure that I have several uninterrupted hours whenever I sit down to write, so this can happen. Whenever a story like this is in progress, it is so exciting that I will do almost anything to get those hours—break appointments, call in sick, tell lies. I become a person on drugs, somebody in the throes of a passionate affair. I'll do anything to get there, to make it happen again. I know I can't ignore the voice, or waste it. I may be a fool, but I'm not that kind of a fool.

Since the writing of fiction is such a physical and personal process for me, I have to write in longhand, still. I have to write with a pen or pencil on a legal pad. I can't have anything mechanical between my body and the page. Later, I'll type it on a computer in order to revise. I can compose nonfiction directly on the computer, but not fiction. Perhaps it's because fiction is so messy, like life. Often I jot down three or four words before I hit upon the right one—or I hope it's the right one. So I mark all the others out, and go on writing, but I want to keep them all, all those words I thought about first and then discarded. I also want to keep that paragraph of description I marked out, and that earlier section about how Ray drowned the dog when he was eleven, and that chapter from the point of view of the mother, because I might change my mind later on and include them. The novel, at this point, is organic, living, changing; anything can still happen, and probably will. This is true up until the very moment when I print the whole thing out and put it into its little coffin, usually an old paper box. Then I hit that SEND button and it's gone to the publisher. Then it's dead, they're all dead, all those people who have been my familiars, who have lived under my skin for weeks and months or years, and I am no longer a writer, but a murderer and mourner, infinitely more alone in the world.

WRITING CAN ALSO GIVE US the chance to express what is present but mute, or unvoiced, in our own personalities . . .

because we are all much more complicated and various people than our lives allow.

During the early eighties, the mountains where I came from began to change rapidly. The fast food restaurants went in around the bend of the Levisa River near my parents' house, for instance, and those satellite TV dishes sprouted like weird mushrooms on every hillside—meaning that the children growing up there wouldn't sound like I do, or like their grandmothers did, but like Walter Cronkite instead. That's when I began to tape my relatives and elderly mountain friends, collecting the old stories, songs, and histories in earnest, with the aim of preserving the type of speech—Appalachian English—and the ways of life of a bygone era. But then a very strange thing happened to me. In *Oral History*, the first novel I wrote using this material exclusively, a voice began speaking who was truly me, in a way in which all these other, more contemporary, and ostensibly autobiographical characters were not—although she (Granny Younger, an old mountain midwife) was certainly more removed from me in time, and place, and circumstance, than any other character I'd ever come up with.

Here is what she says in the first chapter of my novel *Oral History*:

. . . I'll tell it all directly.

I'll tell it all, but don't you forget it is Almarine's story. Almarine's, and Pricey Jane's, and Lord yes, it's that red-headed Emmy's. Mought be it's her story moren the rest. Iffen twas my story, I never would tell it at all. There's tales I'll tell, and tales I won't. And iffen twas my story, why I'd be all hemmed in by the facts of it like Hoot Owl Holler is hemmed in by them three mountains. I couldn't move no way but forward. And often in my traveling over these hills I have seed that what you want the most, you find offen the beaten path. I never find nothing I need on the trace, for an instance. I never find ary a thing. But I am an old, old woman, and I have traveled a lot in these parts. I have seed folks come and I have seed them go. I have cotched more babies than I can name you; I have put the bury-ing quilts around many a soul. I said I know moren you know and mought be I'll tell you moren you want to hear. I'll tell you a story that's truer than true, and nothing so true is so pretty. It's blood on the moon, as I said. The way I tell a story is the way I want to, and iffen you mislike it, you don't have to hear.

Granny Younger is expressing that part of me that is the writer part, that knows things I don't know, and that does not find its expression in any other role I perform—as mother, wife, or teacher, for instance.

Writing has become a source of strength for me, too. I had barely begun a novel named *Fair and Tender Ladies*—intended as an honest account and a justification, really, of the lives of so many resourceful mountain women I'd grown up among, women whose plain and home-centered lives are not much val-ued in the world at large—when my beloved mother went into her last illness, a long and drawn-out sequence of falls, emphysema, and finally heart failure. This period coincided with the onset of Josh's schizophrenia; I spent two years visiting hospitals, sitting by hospital beds, often reading students' work as I tried to hold on to my teaching job. I don't know what I would have done if I hadn't been writing that novel. I worked on it a bit every day; it was like an open door to another world, another place for me to be for a little while.

Its heroine, Ivy Rowe, grew stronger and stronger, the more I needed her. Every terrible thing in the world happened to her—extreme poverty, too many children, heartbreak, illness, the death of a child—but she could take it. She hung in there, so I did, too. Ivy made sense of her life through writing a constant stream of letters: to her children, to her friends, to her sisters—especially to her favorite sister, Silvaney, even though Silvaney had died young and would never read most of them. Near the novel's end, Ivy burns all her letters, and it is finally my own voice as well as hers that concludes:

. . . The smoke from the burning letters rose and was lost in the clouds. . . . With every one I burned, my soul grew lighter, lighter, as if it rose too with the smoke. And I was not even cold, long as I'd been out there. For I came to understand something in that moment . . . which I had never understood in all these years.

The letters didn't mean anything.

Not to the dead girl Silvaney, of course—*nor to me.*

Nor had they ever.

It was the *writing* of them, that signified.

In 2003 I had done a lot of historical research but had barely begun a novel named *On Agate Hill* when Josh died. My grief—and rage—were indescribable: "oceanic," to use one doctor's terminology. He told me that there are basically two physiological reactions to grief. Some people sleep a lot, gain weight, become depressed and lethargic.

I had the other reaction—I felt like I was standing with my finger stuck into an electrical outlet, all the time. I couldn't sleep. I couldn't read, I couldn't eat, I couldn't remember anything, anything at all. I forgot how to drive to the grocery store. I couldn't find the school where I had taught for twenty years. In group situations, I was apt to blurt out wildly inappropriate remarks, like a person with Tourette's syndrome. I cried all the time. I lost thirty pounds.

Weeks passed, then months. I was wearing out my husband and my friends. But I couldn't calm down. It was almost as if I had become addicted to these days on fire, to this intensity. I felt that if I lost it, I'd lose him even more.

Finally I started going to a psychiatrist, a kind, rumpled man who formed his hands into a little tent and listened to me scream and cry and rave for several weeks.

Then came the day when he held up his hand and said, "Enough."

"What?" I stared at him.

"I am going to give you a new prescription," my psychiatrist said, taking out his pad and pen. He began to write.

"Oh good," I said, wanting more drugs, anything.

He ripped the prescription out and handed it to me.

"Write fiction every day," it said in his crabbed little hand.

I just looked at him.

"I have been listening to you for some time," he said, "and it has occurred to me that you are an extremely lucky person, since you are a writer, because it is possible for you to enter into a narrative not your own, for extended periods of time. To live in someone else's story, as it were. I want you to do this every day for two hours. I believe that it will be good for you."

"I can't," I said. "I haven't written a word since Josh died."

"Do it," he said.

"I can't think straight, I can't concentrate," I said.

"Then just sit in the chair," he said. "Show up for work."

Vocational rehabilitation, I thought. Like Josh. So I did it. For three days. The fourth day, I started to write.

And my novel, which I'd planned as the diary of a young girl orphaned by the Civil War, just took off and wrote itself. "I know I am a spitfire and a burden," Molly Petree begins on May 20, 1874. "I do not care. My family is a dead family, and this is not my home, for I am a refugee girl . . . but evil or good I intend to write it all down every true thing in black and white upon the page, for evil or good it is my own true life and I WILL have it. I will."

Molly's spitfire grit strengthened me as she proceeded to "give all her heart," no matter what, during a passionate life journey that included love, betrayal, motherhood, and grief (of course, grief). But by the time we were done with it, Molly and I, two years later, she had finally found a real home, and I could find my way to the grocery store. I could laugh. And yes, through the mysterious alchemy of fiction, my sweet Josh had managed to find his own way into the final pages of the novel after all, as a mystical bluesman and healer living wild and free at last in the deep piney woods he used to play in as a child.

When Joan Didion published *My Year of Magical Thinking*, with its close observation of her life during the painful year following her husband's death, a friend wondered, "How can she do that—write at such a time?"

"The right question is, how could she *not* do that?" I answered. Writing is what Joan Didion does, it's what she has always done. It's how she has lived her life.

In a different way, I realized, this is how I have lived my life, too. Of course writing is an escape, but it is a source of nourishment and strength, too. My psychiatrist's prescription may benefit us all. Whether we are writing fiction or nonfiction, journaling or writing for publication, writing itself is an inherently therapeutic activity. Simply to line up words one after another upon a page is to create some order where it did not exist, to give a recognizable shape to the chaos of our lives. Writing cannot bring our loved ones back, but it can sometimes fix them in our fleeting memories as they were in life, and it can always help us make it through the night.

Angels Passing

DO WE EVER GET BEYOND the images of childhood? The way we first hear language, for instance (old women on a porch, talking on and on as it gets dark) or how Mama smells (loose powder, cigarettes, Chanel No5). Or in particular, Christmas: my Aunt Bess's quivery soprano on "O Holy Night" in the chilly stone church. The sharp strange smell of grapefruit, shipped from Florida in a wooden crate. The guns of Christmas morning, echoing around and around the ring of frosty mountains. How the air smells right before it snows, and how the sky looks, like the underside of a quilt. Oranges studded with cloves, in a bowl on a coffee table. The blazing fires in the oil drums as we go screaming down Hoot Owl Holler on our sleds ("sleigh-riding," we call it), then get hauled back up the mountain in the back of somebody's truck to do it all over again. My daddy in his dimestore wearing a red bow tie. All my images of the holiday season cluster around the dimestore, the Methodist Church, and my mama's winter kitchen, which was always filled with people and food.

It seemed like everybody in the whole world dropped by to sit a spell and see what she was up to. And sure enough there she was, wearing a pretty apron over a pretty dress (Mama was the kind of woman who dressed up every day), turning out batch after batch of her famous fudge. She'd already made the fruitcakes, of course, and now they sat in the "cold corner," drenched in rum. (Does anybody really like fruitcake? I doubt it. But fruitcake at Christmas was the law.) Sherry pound cakes, sugar cookies, and pecan pies got wrapped in tin foil, then tied up in bows. If the back doorbell rang, it would be a man named George or a man named Arnold, drunk and wanting money, which I got to give them if my Mama had her hands in some kind of dough, which she usually did.

My parents gave lots of presents; Daddy was always worried about giving everybody "enough." Besides their many friends, we were surrounded by relatives—they lived on either side of us and up the road from our house in the Levisa River bottom, and all over town. Delivering the gifts took three days, because of course Mama and I had to sit and talk for a while at every house we went to. Daddy used to order oysters at Christmastime, especially for Mama. The wooden barrel of oysters, packed in ice, came all the way across Virginia from Chincoteague Island. We went down to the station for days on end, meeting every Norfolk and Western train, looking for them. When they finally arrived, it took several men to carry them to our house. A mining engineer who'd been born in South Carolina came over to open them. A couple of women were waiting to help Mama cook. They worked on the oysters for two days, and on the evening of the second day, just about everybody in town showed up to help eat them. We had oysters in the shell, fried in cracker meal, in fritters, in stew, and scalloped. Everyone was fascinated; most of the townspeople had never even heard of oysters before "Miss Gig" moved to town. As old Dr. Burkes said, arranging a red bandana over his fancy three-piece suit, "I'd like to know who was the first man that ever thought to eat such a monstrosity as this!" Like the fruitcakes, the oysters were mainly something to put up with, in my opinion. What I liked was the ambrosia and the floating island for dessert.

We ate holiday dinners at the big round table in the dining room at my grandparents' house, with Grandmother presiding blue-haired and ethereal above the snowy linen. I used to drop my napkin on purpose just to lean down and look at the huge dark claws on the pedestal base of the table—cruel, strong, and evil, evil. I'd come up flushed and thrilled.

Christmas was a time for cousins, who'd arrive next door from southside Virginia with such long names that it'd take their mother forever to call them in out of the snow—"Martha Fletcher Bruce! Anne Vicars Bruce!" My relationship with my pretty redheaded first cousins Randy and Melissa was more complicated. I liked them, but mainly I wanted to *be* them . . . to belt out "I Enjoy Being a Girl" the way Melissa did in the Rotary Talent Show, to be as smart and exemplary as Randy. It was clear that Jesus liked her better than me.

I aspired to sainthood in those days. I might have settled for a little miracle, or a vision, or at least a sign. I remember one Christmas Eve staring fixedly at Missy, my Pekingese, for hours, because a granny-woman had told me that God speaks through animals on Christmas Eve. He didn't say a word through Missy. But never mind, I was all eaten up with holiness anyway, excited by the holly in the church, the candles, the carols, and the Christmas pageant, which we acted out at the altar year after year, wearing our bathrobes, until we were too old to be in it. There were not enough boys in that little church, so I usually had to be a Wise Man, while Randy and Melissa and Frances Williams got to be the angels. I wanted to be an angel so bad. But would I ever fit through the eye of the needle? Didn't I have too much stuff?

At school we drew names and I gave gifts to kids from up in the hollers, saving my allowance to buy them the nicest things—Evening in Paris perfume, Avon dusting powder, a pen and pencil set in a clear plastic case. In return I got a hooked potholder once, and a red plastic barrette, and a terrific homemade slingshot. On snowy nights around Christmas I used to sit out by myself for hours, hearing the wild dogs bark way up in the mountains, listening hard for the high, sweet song of angels. I never heard it, either. When my daddy came home from the dimestore, I'd finally go in the house.

He never left on Christmas Eve until the store was closed, cash counted and put in the safe, the last layaway doll picked up—and if somebody couldn't pay, which happened often enough when the mines weren't working, he'd give it away. In early October, I'd go with him to the Ben Franklin Toy Fair in Baltimore, where we'd order presents for Christmas. I was the doll consultant.

In those days, in that town, it was a sin to sell on the Sabbath; but from Thanksgiving until Christmas, every Sunday, I got to go downtown to "work" in the dimestore, helping Daddy and the "girls" fix things up for the week ahead. As doll consultant, I'd dust the dolls and fluff up their dresses and stand them up just so . . . I particularly liked to raise their arms a bit, so they'd be ready to hug any little girl they got on Christmas morning.

Weren't these Christmases idyllic? Wasn't my childhood wonderful? Yes and no. It's like those awful claws beneath the festive table at my grandmother's house. For there were terrible resentments and quarrels about money and old unhealed wounds right beneath the surface in that family, as in all families. Somebody was always going off to "take the cure," while others were "kindly nervous." In the parlance of today, our family was dysfunctional (is any family not?)

I would never become an angel, or even a saint. Instead I

would grow up wild, marry young, and settle down. We'd have two boys, forming our own dysfunctional family. We'd do the best we could. Then we'd divorce, and I'd feel "kindly nervous" myself. I'd remarry. I'd try like crazy. (We all do, don't we? We try like crazy.) My new, husband and I would form our own new, blended dysfunctional family. And even now that we've been married for thirty years, I realize how hard divorce always is for kids, no matter what those self-help books say. Though the kids are all grown up now, they lost some big bright pieces out of their childhoods, out of their lives.

For I could never give them what I had: my father in a red bowtie standing forever in front of his dimestore; my mother forever in her kitchen wearing Fire and Ice lipstick and high heels; the cousins next door and across the street; Jesus right up the road in the little stone Methodist Church.

The church is a parking lot now. The dimestore is gone. Walmart looms over the river. I'm seventy, an age that has brought no wisdom. When I was young, I always thought the geezers knew some things I didn't; the sad little secret is, we don't. I don't understand anything anymore, though I'm still in there, still trying like crazy.

We do what we can, don't we? Before Christmas, I still make fudge, party mix, sherry pound cakes, and sugar cookies. With four small grandchildren, our holiday plans vary now. We go where the children are. I always make a trip to Nashville to visit Lucy and Spencer Seay right around Christmastime.

Last year, our granddaughter Ellery Ferguson was chosen to play Mary in an Episcopal church pageant in Raleigh. Her younger sister Baker was First Donkey. On Christmas Eve, I still make scalloped oyster casserole. But sometime on Christmas Day—around the tree or at the table—there will come a moment when the conversation spontaneously ceases while we pause, and remember. One of those little silences that sometimes fall upon us all—angels passing.

The Little Locksmith

I wake early here, in our corner bedroom already flooded with light. Beyond the window, light winks on the shining water of Penobscot Bay and glows through the mist that still shrouds Islesboro and Belfast and the Camden Hills beyond; light rolls golden down the sloping yard to the water. I'm instantly wide awake, so wide awake it's scary. I get up immediately, pull on some jeans and sneakers, go downstairs, feed Betty the dog, and together we walk out through the tall, dewy grass and down the wooden steps to the rocky shore, which changes with every high tide. The birch trees rustle in their papery, conspiratorial way. Birds cry out. Little white waves break on the shore. But this water is cold, not like the Myrtle Beach or Wrightsville Beach of my youth, where you could jump the waves all day and they would pick you up and hold you in their warm, salty embrace. No, this water would kill you; you have to enter and exit quickly, shivering. There's no boardwalk, no dance pavilion, no Krispy Kreme doughnut place. It's beautiful here, but it's a severe, rigorous beauty. A loon calls across the water. Light leaps off the little waves like a thousand arrows aimed at me; I fish my sunglasses out of my pocket and put them on, though it isn't even 7 a.m. yet. I breathe deeply in this chilly air, which seems strangely effervescent, like breathing champagne.

And actually I'm feeling a little intoxicated, the way I often feel here, the way I always feel when I'm starting a new novel, which I am—or will, as soon as I get up my nerve. It's that old disorientation, that scary lightness of being, that moment before you spring off the diving board straight out into the shining air, head first. You could kill yourself, and you know it, and you've got to get to the point where you don't care.

I'm not quite there yet.

But by fortunate chance, I'm here in Castine, a place I associate with taking risks and writing. Nobody's home but me and an old dog and an accommodating husband who doesn't care how crazy I act when I'm starting a novel. So I don't even leave him a note when I take Betty back inside and grab up my windbreaker and gulp down two Advils because I have a long hill to climb now and I've got a bad knee which is par for the course when you're old, which I am. This is a true thing I have only recently discovered and it is like an ugly scab someplace on my body I never noticed before but now I can't quit picking at it. Finally I open my book bag and take out my current copy of *The Little Locksmith*, by Katharine Butler Hathaway. I've given away at least a dozen copies of this book since it was republished by the Feminist Press, after Maine writer Alix Kates Shulman found it in a secondhand bookstore and brought it to their attention. It first came to me here, years back, when I really needed it—as books so often do. Since then it has become my talisman, my Bible, my lucky charm.

I give it mostly to my sister writers (because it is one of the best books ever written about writing) but also to anyone suffering adversity of any sort, especially any kind of illness or disability, for it is truly a story of transformation, one of the finest spiritual autobiographies ever written. Basically I give it to people I love, trusting that it will mean as much to them as it has to me. As Katharine herself says (I'm going to call her Katharine in this essay since I consider her my true friend), hers was "a lonely voyage of discovery" that began when she decided that she "couldn't let fear decide things" for her, when she decided "to follow the single, fresh living voice" of her "own destiny." Indeed this is a fearless book, as well as an entirely original one. It is not at all like anything else I have ever read. Though she was very frail, Katharine was tough as nails, intellectually; wielding her pen with a jeweler's precision, she crafted this book like an exquisitely cut jewel—a topaz, I think, rather than a diamond (maybe I think this since it's my own birthstone, but everybody who reads this books wants to claim it as her own). Each facet reveals a new insight or an indelible image. Hold it up to the window, turn it this way and that, and it will cast off rays of light in every direction, piercing even the oddest, most secret depths of the reader's psyche. *The Little Locksmith* tells the story of how Katharine overcame her severe physical and psychological handicaps (her "predicament," she calls it) and came to this tiny, out-of-the-way village on Maine's stern rocky coast where, against her family's wishes and all advice, she bought a house on Court Street, overlooking the harbor.

I'm headed there now. I give Betty a biscuit, close the front door softly, and walk out our leafy lane, turning right onto the main road. I walk through swirling ground mist across the old British Canal, then climb up the long, steep curve into town. Katharine's book fits easily in the pocket of my windbreaker; it's a small book, like its author.

Born in 1890 into a loving, prosperous family in Salem, Massachusetts, Katharine Butler Hathaway was stricken with spinal tuberculosis at age five and "changed from a rushing, laughing child into a bedridden, meditative one." The most advanced medical theories of the day dictated her new "horizontal life," which would last for ten years. "For the doctor's treatment consisted in my being strapped down very tight on a stretcher, on a very hard sloping bed, with my shoulders pressed against a hard pad. My head was kept from sinking down on my chest . . . by means of a leather halter attached to a rope which went through a pulley at the head of the bed. On the end of the rope hung a five-pound iron weight. This mechanism held me a prisoner for twenty-four hours a day, without the freedom to turn or twist my body or let my chin move out of its up-tilted position in the leather halter, except to go from side to side. My back was supposed to be kept absolutely still." However, Katharine's "hands and arms and mind were free. . . . I held my pencil and pad of paper up in the air above my face, and I wrote microscopic letters and poems, and made little books of stories, and very tiny pictures" along with paper dolls, dollhouse furniture, and doll clothes. In these Brontë-like pursuits she was accompanied always by her loving brothers and sister, who "took it for granted that no other amusement was really interesting compared with drawing or writing or making something" and made her bedroom "the natural center of the house for the others."

Yet her natural "happy, sparkling" sense of herself was challenged by the "ghoulish pleasure" of visiting children who stared at her halter and strap, and by their parents' overt pity. Worst of all was the occasional appearance of the hunchback who came to the house to fix locks. Katharine had been told that without the treatment she would have grown up to be like him. Yet she felt the "truth was that I really belonged with him, even if it was never going to show. I was secretly linked with him, and I felt a strong, childish, amorous pity and desire toward him, so that there was even a queer erotic charm for me about his gray shabby clothes, the strange awful peak in his back, and his cross,

unapproachable sadness which made him not look at other people, not even me lying on my bed and staring sideways at him."

When Katharine was finally released from her board at fifteen, this suspicion was, alas, confirmed: "That person in the
mirror couldn't be me! I felt inside like a healthy, ordinary lucky
person.... A hideous disguise had been cast over me." Katharine's
refusal to accept her limitations—including her desire for sexual love, which shocked many readers when this book was first
published in 1943—strikes me as an act of great courage. She
always "believed passionately that every human being could be
happy," including herself.

She was admitted to Radcliffe College, where she spent
three blissful years as a special student and made several good
friends for life: smart, artistic, bohemian girls among whom
she flourished in her "perfect imitation of a grown-up person,
one who was noted for a sort of peaceful wise detachment,"
whose "curious, impersonal life gave her an enviable agelessness
and liberty." But this self fell apart when she returned home
after college. She fell into deep depression and "toxic fear" (ag-
oraphobia), a complete disintegration from which she finally
emerged through her old childhood pastime, writing.

"A block of paper and a pencil had saved me. They had not
only saved me by satisfying my hunger and canceling the over-
whelming terror of the universe, but they gave me also an in-
exhaustible form of entertainment because they gave me, or

seemed to give me, the equivalent of all sorts of human experience. There was no end and no limit to this kind of living." Her writing restored "the greatest visible world" to her as "an object of love, full of mystery and meaning." Thus she "got hold of a most extraordinary joy."

Katharine's transformation was further accomplished by buying the house I'm standing in front of right now, atop this windy hill. When an unexpected legacy allowed her to conceive her grand plan of living independently, she first thought she'd buy "a thimble . . . something *mignonne* and doll-like," just like herself: "a very small childish spinster . . . a little oddity, deformed and ashamed and shy." Instead, she found herself "awestruck by the force of destiny" when she came upon this "very large high square house on Penobscot Bay overlooking the Bagaduce River and the islands and the Cape Rosier Hills. . . . I knew that whether I liked it or not this at last was my house."

Somebody else lives in Katharine's house now, of course, and yet it's all here, just as she described it: the bright sun, the endless wind, the flower-studded fields dropping down to the harbor. It's easy to imagine her sitting on this wide stone doorsill, "rapturously at home," as she often sat that first summer while workmen hammered and painted and restored the chimneys, the twelve-paned windows, the "old heavy original door" whose "panels, set with narrow, handmade moldings, made a great serene sign of the cross—two short panels at the top and two tall ones below." Indeed it is still the "sober, grand, romantic house" that was to be her "rebellion against cuteness. . . . I wanted room to find out what I really was, and room to be whatever I really was." *The Little Locksmith* is the story of how Katharine grew to fit her house, shedding her self-identity as a cripple and assuming her true identity as artist.

Katharine's transformation, her "new world," is described in terms of light: "I had never seen a world so gilded and so richly bathed and blessed by such a benign sun as that world was by that sun. The sun seemed to pour down a lavish, golden, invulnerable contentment on everything, on people, houses, animals, fields—and a sweetness like the sweetness of passion." Which would come to her, too, against all odds, in "that graceful sitting room, full of sunshine, on the southwest corner, the room destined to become the one most used and most loved of the entire house. Wonderful, strange things happened to me and were said to me there, which I never could have believed were possible at the time when I was so eagerly preparing it."

Eventually, Katharine left this house and found her way to Paris, where she became part of a vibrant circle of friends, writers, and artists. "Everything is different since Castine. Yet it all began there. For there and then I first began in utter ignorance and naïveté and to heed the little voice which spoke to me and told me which way to turn." Eventually Katharine came to believe that this was in fact the voice of God; she wrote that *The*

Little Locksmith was "going to be my bread-and-butter letter to God, for a lovely visit on the earth." Her happiness was complete when she fell in love with Dan Hathaway of Marblehead, Massachusetts, marrying him in 1932. Though the Depression forced them to sell Katharine's beloved house, perhaps it had already served its purpose; the couple ended up blissfully happy in a "smaller and cozier" house in Blue Hill, Maine—just up the peninsula from Castine.

Chapters of *The Little Locksmith* were being serially published in *The Atlantic Monthly* magazine in the fall of 1942—to great acclaim and national interest—when Katharine's precarious health "went haywire." "At present," she wrote from the Blue Hill Hospital in early December, "my only comfortable posture is on the knees with head bent down in front of me, like a snail or an unborn child. Only then can I breathe." She died on Christmas Eve. *The Little Locksmith* was published posthumously the following year. Writing it meant everything to her ("I love this book and I can hardly bear to leave it now" she wrote at the end); its publication seemed almost irrelevant.

And yet it's still here. This book is in my pocket. This house is still here on its hill, everything just as Katharine described it: the fanlight over the heavy door; the twelve-paneled windows; the brick path, lovingly uncovered; the swaying willows; and most of all, the light. The entire "great visible world" is here before us, our own real world, where amazing things are possible.

It's all still here for us all, if we can overcome our fears and summon the courage to trust ourselves, to listen to whatever voice speaks within us, to trust Katharine's "magic of transformation." I check my watch: seven forty-five. There's still time to walk back down the hill, make some coffee for my husband, if he hasn't done it already, and maybe—who knows? start a novel.

ACKNOWLEDGMENTS

Since these essays are drawn from every part of my life, there's no end to the people I'd like to thank—so many that I'm scared to make a big list for fear of leaving anyone out. So here I will try to acknowledge those who have contributed most to the actual writing of *Dimestore*. First comes my old friend Debbie Raines, senior English teacher at Grundy High School, whose insights and on-the-scene commentary have been invaluable to me, as was the time I spent working with her students to publish our oral history of downtown Grundy, *Sitting on the Courthouse Bench*, in 2000 (Tryon Publishing Co., Inc., Chapel Hill). My longtime editor Shannon Ravenel (recently retired) offered initial enthusiasm and some shrewd judgments at the outset of this project; my present editor Kathy Pories brought close editing and a much needed sense of order and shape to this collection. I also want to thank Mona Sinquefield, friend and secretary, who suffered through version after version, draft after draft; Chris Stamey, the best copy editor in the world; Brunson Hoole, whose sleight of hand somehow turns all this stuff into an actual book; art designer Anne Winslow; and too many other people at Algonquin to name, starting with publisher Elisabeth Scharlatt, Ina Stern, Craig Popelars, and the whole wonderful publicity team. It's such a pleasure to work with you all. I'm indebted to sister writers and early readers Frances Mayes and Marianne Gingher, who came up with great ideas and suggestions. Big thanks go out to my special support group of "Good Ol' Girls"—Jill McCorkle, Marshall Chapman, and Matraca Berg. To my beloved friend Elizabeth Spencer, always an inspiration, and to the wonderful and steadfast Liz Darhansoff, who has been my agent practically since we were girls. Special thanks to the Hindman Settlement School in Hindman, Kentucky, where I have spent so much valuable time over the past thirty years. My essay "Lightning Storm" honors the people I was privileged to know during my three years working in the literacy programs at Hindman's adult learning center. I also want to thank all my Grundy and southwest Virginia relatives, especially my father's business partner and best friend, Curtis E. Smith, his son Jack Smith, and Steve Smith, now CEO of the Food City stores, which have benefited so many in southwest Virginia, for their constant support always and especially their loving care of my parents during their later years. Thanks to Ava McClanahan for this as well as being a constant source of lore and stories all my life. Love and apologies for general ditziness during the writing of this book go to my children Page Seay and Amity Crowther, and always, always, to Hal.